God's Redeeming Story

(a theological primer)

Merle D. Strege
Richard L. Willowby

Bridges

Warner Press Ministries
Anderson, Indiana

All scripture passages, unless otherwise indicated, are from the King James Version, the Revised Standard Version, © copyright, 1972, Thomas Nelson, the New Revised Standard Version of the Bible, copyright ©1989 by the Division of Christian Education of the National Council of the Churches of Christ in the USA, or the Holy Bible, New International Version. Copyright © 1973, 1978, 1984 International Bible Society. Used by permission of Zondervan Bible Publishers.

© 1996 by Warner Press, Inc
ISBN #0-87162-668-3   Stock #D-5601
UPC# 730817 05601 2

David C. Shultz, Editor in Chief
Arthur M. Kelly, BRIDGES Book Editor
Cover by Larry Stuart

Dedicated to
Carol Schmidt
and to the memories of
Vernon "Smitty" Schmidt
and
John and Bessie Willowby

Contents

God's Redeeming Story

(A THEOLOGICAL PRIMER)

Tell me the old, old story,
Of Jesus and His love.

0.0 An Introduction

This book is a companion to BRIDGES, the church school curriculum published by Warner Press Ministries, a division of Warner Press, the Publication Board of the Church of God. An appropriate phrase to describe the book's purpose is *theological primer*. Written for church school workers and others interested in the study of the Bible, it explores some of the Bible's major theological themes, as well as its role, history, and importance in the life of the church. As a companion to BRIDGES this book is intended to help church school teachers see their work as a calling. That calling encourages Christians to be grounded in the Bible and formed by its great narrative, that is, God's search for and calling of a people who live faithfully to God for the sake of the world's redemption. It need not, however, be restricted to that purpose. Some readers may wish to use this book as a guide to the study of

1

basic themes of the church's theology. In fact, we hope that many will find it useful as a basic introduction to biblical theology.

The primary ministries of the church are two: evangelism—the preaching of Jesus in fulfillment of the Great Commission so that "all may be saved"; and discipleship—teaching those in the church so that they may more fully know "the mind of Christ" (Phil 2:5), and so that they, like their Lord, may daily increase "in wisdom and in years and in divine and human favor" (Luke 2:52).

The teaching ministry of the church resides, finally and importantly, in the hearts, minds, and skills of the church's teachers as well as in the church's curriculum. Curriculum is a map, a guide, and a direction. As important as it is, the teacher is the key to the nurturing, discipleship-oriented classroom. Therefore, this book is written with the teacher in mind. It is a resource to enable the teacher to better enable the students.

Since this book is meant to accompany BRIDGES and since that curriculum is centered in the Bible, we will first look at some basic questions that readers may have about the Bible and the approach we intend to take toward it here. We will attempt to answer those questions by referring both to the theological history of the Church of God movement and some of the work of more recent biblical scholarship.

0.1 Overview

Since the Bible may be regarded as a great narrative concerning God, Israel, Jesus, and the church, this text is organized around those four major biblical topics as well as the Bible itself. In the chapters that follow we hope to integrate the narrative structure of scripture with the theological themes of the Warner Press church school curriculum, BRIDGES. In the process you, the teacher, as well as other readers, will gain some insight into the theological motifs of the Bible and the Christian tradition. This should help you to enable the discipleship of the learners in your church school class.

You will find this book, then, divided into five chapters. None of these is exhaustive, but each generally discusses its subject in relation to the five themes or perspectives around which BRIDGES has been developed:

- Life and Its Setting
- Revelation
- Redemption
- The Christian Community, and
- Discipleship

Chapter one presents a discussion of issues and concepts about the Bible—its history, the questions of inspiration and authority, and its relationship to the believing community. The chapter on God, chapter two, does not pretend to hold all that can be said about God. It does attempt, however, to discuss the topic of God in relation to the themes of redemption, revelation, and the corporate people of God—whether Israel or the church—as they are displayed in the Bible. Similarly, chapter three will consider the topic of Israel in relation to the themes of the life of discipleship and the nature of the community that God calls into being and into relationship with God. The subject matter of chapters two and three is drawn largely from the Old Testament, although they will refer to the New Testament where warranted by the material. Chapter four deals with Jesus and considers his life and ministry in connection with the themes of redemption, revelation, and discipleship. Finally, chapter five discusses the nature of the Christian community and the life of discipleship.

Additionally, all chapters speak to the overarching theme of "Life and Its Setting." Readers might think of this theme as the element of our discussion that attempts to deal with the perennial question of Bible teachers and students alike: "What does this discussion mean in the daily life situations in which we find ourselves, and how does that situation affect our reading and interpretation of the text?"

From time to time the text will be interrupted by *Implications for Teaching.* These sections are designed to separate and emphasize aspects of this book that are central to the role of the teacher in the classroom. If the teacher serves as the church's educator, then the meaning of a given text must be applied to the classroom. These "implications" are not "how to" implications, but are presented to provoke the teacher's thinking about his or her role in the classroom. In one sense, these implications ask, "If God is this kind of God, what does that have to do with *what* I teach, *whom* I teach, and *how* I teach?"

0.2 Understandings and Usages

We follow one usage in particular that requires explanation at the very outset. Many of our readers will note our use of "Yahweh" as the name of God rather than the more familiar "Jehovah." Our use follows the language of standard biblical scholarship on this subject. The four Hebrew consonants that, translated into English, spell the name of God are YHWH (or sometimes YHVH). Since Hebrew is written only in consonants, readers must supply vowels. The name Jehovah is an earlier assumed pronunciation of the name of God based on an artificial combination of the consonants YHWH with the vowels of another name for God, *Adonai* (the Lord). Old Testament scribes later wrote manuscripts that supplied the vowel points of Adonai between the consonants of Yahweh. "When the vowels of Adonai are combined with the consonants YHWH/YHVH, the form 'Yehovah' results. Since many languages, such as German, use the letter *j* in place of *y*, the form 'Jehovah' resulted. There is no evidence that the personal name of the Israelite deity was ever pronounced Jehovah in antiquity."* On this evidence we will follow what has become the standard reference to the name of God and use the term Yahweh.

0.3 Systematic and Biblical Theology

In a broad sense, theology means talk about God or the study of God. Therefore, anytime persons engage in conversation about God, no matter how casual, they are "doing" theology. Dinner table conversation, Sunday school classes, sermons, dormitory "gab" sessions, worship, prayer, songs, formal seminary, college, and university classes—all are theological discourse as long as the focus is God and God's relationship with humankind and the larger created world.

This book is a book of theology. It is more formal and thoughtful, perhaps, than a dorm session or dinner table talk, but it is concerned with the same matter: to better understand who God is and what is expected of the people of God.

People can "do" theology with many different approaches. They can understand it in many different ways. Most approaches, however, fit into one of two larger categories: systematic theology and biblical theology.

0.31 Systematic Theology is an approach that is an effort to arrange the discussion into an order that helps the student to understand better and more fully what comes before and what comes after any given point of discussion. It is distinguished from biblical theology because a systematic theology will address issues that are not addressed in the Bible. Systematic theologians attempt to "fill in" by inference (probability) or deduction (logic) where the Bible is silent. For example, the Bible does not present a *theogony*, that is, a statement about the origin of God. It begins with the assumption that God is. It makes no attempt to say more than this or to address the question, "Where did God come from?" A systematic theology will offer a theory about that, or enlarge on the idea of God's "origin-less" state.

0.32 Biblical Theology, on the other hand, is quiet when the Bible is quiet. If the Bible is silent about God's origins, biblical theology is also silent. If the Bible offers no explanation about the manner in which sin is transmitted throughout humankind, biblical theology remains silent. Biblical theology seeks to understand the meaning of an "origin-less" God and the meaning and reality of sin, but that would be its limit.

BRIDGES CURRICULUM is a planned guide to the study of the Bible. It links God's word to the human condition, to our condition. *God's Redeeming Story* is designed to assist the teacher in achieving that singularly important goal. Therefore, *God's Redeeming Story* is biblical theology.

0.33 Common Theology. From time to time we will make reference to the phrase *common theology*. This phrase refers to a theology that is widely believed and defended but is not necessarily true to scripture. Much of what passes in churchly discourse today is shaped by persons who have built a ministry on a one-dimensional approach to defining the Christian life. One such current idea, for example, is the significant emphasis on prosperity and success as evidences of the favor of God. This is found as a steady and consistent theme in the preaching and teaching of many "television evangelists." While it is true that prosperity and success are themes addressed in the Bible, it is equally true that prosperity and success are questioned in the Bible. A common, or "popular," theology would emphasize the one and ignore the other.

As noted often in the text, both Israel and the church have struggled with such one-sided or one dimensional viewpoints—much to their regret.

Acknowledgments

We ought to say here at the beginning that neither of us is a trained expert in biblical studies. One of us worked for nearly two decades in the development of curriculum resources for the church, including BRIDGES CURRICULUM. The other teaches at Anderson University in the field of religious studies, but in the areas of theology and religious history—not biblical studies. Both of us, however, are lifelong students of the Bible and are Sunday school teachers of long standing. We write primarily as teachers for teachers. As teachers and curriculum writers we have a keen interest in the church's educational ministry, especially as that ministry centers in the Bible. We have written not with the technical expertise of the scholar, but with the avid interest of teachers who want to share with other teachers. We desire to help church school classes come to terms with the perennially important question, "How are the insights of the Bible to be applied to everyday life?" Our concerns, therefore, are primarily theological and moral. We have written to give more background on the Bible and its theological themes to those who teach and for the sake of the edification of the church.

This book came into being only through the graciousness and efforts of many people. Strege completed his work on the manuscript during a sabbatical leave from Anderson University and wishes to acknowledge his appreciation to the university for making such leaves available to its faculty.

Without institutional release from the demands of the classroom, much work of potentially great benefit would go undone. Some of the discussions conducted in the pages of this book have been topics in our Bible study classes at North Anderson Church of God and Park Place Church of God respectively. We wish to mention our appreciation for the faithful participation and genial conversation of our class members over the years.

From our very earliest days both of us have benefited from the educational ministries of the Church of God (Anderson). We have been powerfully shaped by *Egermeier's Bible Story Book,* by church school teachers and curriculum, ministers who taught us in "Pastor's Class," youth leaders, and the literature produced by Warner Press for the Christian education of its children and adults. We also are both alumni of Anderson University, née College, and studied at its School of Theology. We gratefully acknowledge the thirst for the Bible stimulated in us during our formative years. We are also thankful for the manner in which that thirst was first satisfied, then stimulated afresh through the disciplined, scholarly study of the Bible by our college and seminary professors, the late Boyce W. Blackwelder, Gustav Jeeninga, George Kufeldt, James Earl Massey, George Ramsey, Sr., Frederick v. Shoot, and the late Marie Strong. We trust that this book keeps faith with the efforts of these people on our behalf, although we know that they each could find herein topics that they would want to discuss a little further with us. Like many of the papers we wrote for each of these fine servants of God and the church, we would probably like a chance for further revision; nevertheless, we enjoyed writing the book much more than the papers.

Friendships play important roles in the writing of many

books, and this one is no exception. In several different settings we have discussed many of the ideas written here with a host of friends. In many cases those conversations taught us some of what we present here. All of these people unfortunately cannot be named here, but our indebtedness to some demands that their names be included here: Arthur M. Kelly, Kenneth F. Hall, Deanna Patrick, Randy Litchfield, Joseph Cookston, Willard Reed, Spencer Spaulding, and Tim Dwyer.

Family members must also be acknowledged, for in many instances we stole time from them to write this book. Thanks, therefore, to Cheryl, Nathan, Laura, and Daniel Willowby, and Fran, Ike, and Pete Strege for giving up time that rightfully belonged to them in order that this book could see the light of day.

We dedicate this book to some members of our family as well. John and Bessie Willowby, Richard's father and mother, were dedicated servants of God and the church whose lives ended tragically in an automobile accident as they journeyed to the funeral of a family member. The church's educational ministry was one of Bessie Willowby's lifelong commitments. It is altogether fitting that we dedicate this book to her memory and to John's also, who often made personal life decisions on the basis of their potential effect on the local congregation. Christians educate others in many ways, sometimes like Bessie in classroom settings, but often through the examples that their lives set before others.

For this reason we wish to dedicate this volume to Merle's father- and mother-in-law, Vernon and Carol Schmidt. "Smitty," as nearly everyone referred to him, and Carol were wonderful examples of the life of Christian faith and hope through the months of his struggle with cancer. Smitty's battle ended just a few days after Easter 1995. Those who were graced by his witness can testify with full hearts to the lessons that he and Carol have taught us as much as did ever a classroom teacher.

The Authors
Pentecost, 1996

---

* *s.v.* Jehovah, *The Dictionary of Bible and Religion,* William H. Grentz, General Editor (Nashville: Abingdon Press, 1986), 522.

Chapter One

The Bible and the Church

—Merle Strege—

The law of the Lord is perfect,
  reviving the soul;
the decrees of the Lord are sure,
  making wise the simple;
the precepts of the Lord are right,
  rejoicing the heart;
the commandment of the Lord is clear,
  enlightening the eyes;
the ordinances of the Lord are true
  and righteous altogether.
More to be desired are they than gold,
  even much fine gold;
sweeter also than honey,
  and drippings of the honeycomb.
                    —Psalm 19:7–10 (NRSV)

1.0 Introduction

The Bible we read today is a composite work, written by many hands over many centuries. Originally written primarily in Hebrew and Greek, the Bible is read today almost exclusively in translation and has been for centuries. Jerome's great Vulgate edition, a Latin translation completed in AD 405, served as the Bible for western Christianity for more than a thousand years. Followers of the English theologian John Wycliffe translated the Vulgate edition into English near the end of the fourteenth century. Several English translations followed, including the so-called Geneva Bible of 1560, the favorite version of the Puritans who settled New England, and the extraordinarily popular Authorized Version (the "King James") of 1611.

These are but a few early examples in a long line of English translations extending all the way to today's New International Version and New Revised Standard Version. Over the centuries hundreds of minds have labored at this exacting and difficult work, reading ancient manuscripts in their original languages, comparing those manuscripts for differing texts, deciding which variant should have preference for translation. The Bible—which Christians often handle rather carelessly—is the result of centuries of sacrificial study, labor, and, sometimes, bloodshed.

1.1 The Canon of Scripture

As our translated English Bible is the work of many hands, so prior to translation and over a significant period of time, many people contributed to the writing and composition of the Old and New Testaments that together make up the Christian Bible. Before the Bible was written, however, it was spoken and even sung. None of the four gospels of the New Testament—Matthew, Mark, Luke, and John—was written before AD 60 at the very earliest. Thus for more than two decades the "gospel" (the word comes from the Old English *godspel* and means "God's story") traveled throughout the Roman world by word of mouth. Only after Paul began corresponding with his new churches did people begin to write the *euangelion* (Greek for "good news"). As the Gospel of Luke opens—"Since many have undertaken to set down an orderly account of the events that have been fulfilled among us, just as they were *handed on to us by those who from the beginning were eyewitnesses* and servants of the word, I too decided ... to write ..." (Luke 1:1–3, emphasis added)—the gospel about Jesus was first spoken, then written.

Elements of the Old Testament were also first spoken and sung. Scholars believe that one of the most ancient passages in the entire Old Testament is the "Song of Miriam" (Exod 15:21), sung in celebration of God's miraculous deliverance of Israel at the Red Sea. The Psalms are poems and songs originally composed to be sung to the accompaniment of musical instruments. Some of the psalms were sung antiphonally by groups located on opposing hilltops. Modern-day Christians find it difficult to believe that people could memorize such lengthy texts as Psalm 119, but we must remember that the skill of writing and the possession of writing materials were not nearly so common in the ancient world. The fact that they were so rare made memorization a necessity.

The oral quality of parts of the Old Testament also appears in the sermons, or "oracles," of Israel's prophets, first spoken in thunderous judgment against the sins of the people. We also find the wisdom tradition of the Bible being composed orally and then handed down orally to succeeding generations. The elders of an Israelite village customarily sat in council, comparing and enlarging their observations about the mystery and operation of all of God's creation. Many of these sayings became proverbs that people took to heart and lived by long before they were collected into the book we call Proverbs. Much of the Bible, in both testaments, was first transmitted through the spoken word.

In time, of course, the books of the Bible were written. They were not the only books important to the religious and moral life of Israel and the church. We have already noted Luke's observation of the "many" who had written accounts of Jesus' life. Some, called "extra-biblical" or "apocryphal" gospels, exist to this day. The Old Testament sometimes mentions writings known to the people of that day but lost to us. Thus 2 Kings refers to a source called *The Book of the Annals of the Kings of Israel*. Over the centuries the people of God, first Israel and then the church, read these literary works for instruction, for worship, for encouragement and consolation. In time some writings rose to greater status and eventually were regarded as authoritative for the life and faith of God's people. The term that signifies this status is "canon," from a Greek word that refers to a carpenter's rule or measuring stick. Writings that have met a standard are thus said to be "canonical."

The Old Testament, sometimes called the Hebrew Bible, was the first of the two testaments to come into canonical form. It is traditionally separated into three divisions: Law [*torah*], Prophets [*nebiim*], and Writings [*ketubim*]. Considered authoritative from the very beginning, the Torah is composed of the first five books of the Bible, Genesis through Deuteronomy. Included in the category of the Prophets are all the books from Joshua through 2 Kings (known as the Former Prophets) except Ruth; the Major Prophets (Isaiah, Jeremiah, and Ezekiel); and the Minor

Prophets (the "Book of the Twelve" that includes all the prophetic writings other than the three major prophets). Together the major and minor prophets are known as the Latter Prophets. The Writings make up the third division of the Hebrew Bible. Its material is the most diverse, containing the poetry of the Psalms, the narrative of Chronicles, and the wisdom of the Proverbs, not to mention all the rest of its varied works. As we have said, Israel took the Torah to be authoritative very early. Little is known of the process by which the other Old Testament books came to be regarded as canonical, but about AD 170 Melito, a Christian bishop in Sardis, listed virtually all of the books of the Old Testament considered to be part of the canon. This is the earliest such list known.

Christians of the New Testament era, especially Gentiles and many Greek-speaking Jews who lived in places other than Jerusalem, did not read the Hebrew Bible. Virtually no non-Jew read Hebrew. The scriptures that they read, and to which the New Testament refers, would have been a Greek translation of the books of the Hebrew Bible known as the Septuagint (abbreviated as *LXX*).

The name comes from a legend that seventy-two men completed the task of translation in seventy-two days; "septuagint" meaning seventy. To the books of the Hebrew Bible the Septuagint translators added several other works. Since these additions are not included in the Hebrew Bible, collectively they have come to be known as the "Apocrypha." At the insistence of the bishop and theologian Augustine, Jerome included the apocrypha in his Vulgate translation and thus they came to be included in the version of the Bible judged canonical by the Catholic church. The Septuagint, in any event, was the Bible commonly used by Greek-speaking

Christians of the first century. In fact, most Old Testament quotations in the books of the New Testament are taken from the Septuagint.

While the first Christians read the Septuagint, they also began writing materials that referred more specifically to the events that centered in Jesus' life, death, and resurrection. The earliest of these materials found in the New Testament are the letters of the Apostle Paul. Others wrote letters of hope, instruction, and exhortation to young congregations and isolated Christians. To these were added narrative accounts of the life of Jesus and the acts of the early church and Christian martyrs. Manuals of procedure for the conduct of church worship and life also appeared before AD 100. As the second Christian century opened, Christians increasingly drew upon a wide range of literature that, in one way or another, centered in the life and teachings of Christ.

Many interpretations of Jesus in circulation during this era conflicted with others. This situation naturally led Christians to question which witnesses to Christ were reliable and authoritative. Their problems were complicated by the presence of fringe members in the Christian movement who published their own lists of authoritative Christian writings. Over a lengthy period of time, certain writings emerged as crucial to the life of the church and the church, not without great conflict and debate, recognized them to be so. The New Testament canon and the Christian church emerged together, each symbiotically shaping the other. As the canon shaped the church, the church recognized and authorized the canon. This reciprocal shaping took place over several centuries until AD 367, when Athanasius, Bishop of Alexandria, published a list of authoritative books naming the twenty-seven books that today comprise the New Testament.

1.2 Authority and Interpretation

Henry C. Wickersham, a late nineteenth and early twentieth century pastor and theologian in the Church of God movement, once published this definition of the authority and inspiration of the Bible:

> The Bible is the only authentic source from which instruction can be derived, in relation to the knowledge of God; his various dispensations to mankind, and the duties required of men by their Creator. As it claims to be regarded as the book of God, a divine authority, so it claims to be the only authority. It is not a rule, it is the rule of faith and practice. The Bible, therefore, is the canon; that is the authoritative standard of salvation and morality.
>
> The different writers of the books of the Bible were inspired of God. It is not the words of the Bible that were inspired, it is not the thoughts of the Bible that were inspired; it is the men who wrote the Bible that were inspired. Inspiration acts not on the man's words, not on the man's thought, but on the man himself; so that he, by his own spontaneity, under the impulse of the Holy Ghost, conceives certain thoughts and gives utterance to them in certain words, both the words and the thoughts receiving the peculiar impress of the mind which conceived and uttered them.[1]

We should pay special attention to the following points in Wickersham's statement: (1) the Bible is authoritative; (2) the Bible is authoritative in matters of Christian theology and morality; (3) the Bible is authoritative and inspired, but not in the sense that God dictated its words to humans who then took them down like ancient stenographers. Rather, the Bible is inspired because it is the product of humans who worked under the "impulse," that is, the inspiration, of the Holy Spirit. Clearly, Wickersham thought that inspiration happened to the people who wrote the Bible. We might say further that inspiration also acts on the people of God, which taken together form the congregation, when they gather to read and interpret the Bible.

Each of these three points needs to be amplified. First, *the Bible is authoritative*. What do we mean to say by this claim? In what sense is the Bible authoritative? Old Testament theologian Walter Brueggemann offers this simple one-sentence description of the Bible: "The Bible is a shared memory of events that were important to our fathers."[2] Much of our understanding of the Bible's authority is conveyed in this sentence. The Bible was not written by just anybody, nor is it a collection of random memories.

Instead, the Bible is the collected narratives and writings based on events that were important to our forefathers and foremothers in the faith. If these people were alive, they would want to teach us "whatever is true ... honorable ... just ... pure ... pleasing ... commendable" (Phil 4:8). Much in the manner of loving parents, these men and women seek through the Bible's pages to nurture the people of God in a particular way of life, to "walk in the way of the Lord," a way formed by devotion to the God of the Bible. This comparison makes distinctions between kinds of authority, and it is important to our discussion to explain exactly which kind of authority we have in mind when we say that the Bible is authoritative.

By way of illustrating the idea of authority that Brueggemann's description of the Bible implies, we might compare it to parental experience. Family life offers an illustration of a kind of authority that we call "authoring." Parents can be appropriately described as the "authors" of their children. They generate children. By their parenting they write plots by which they hope their children's characters will be formed as young men and women of integrity. But most parents also concede that they do not possess the kind of authority that can be employed to force their children to "turn out well."

Rather, parents raise their children in the awareness (and hope, we dare say) that the day will come when sons and daughters will have matured to the point when they make important life choices without direct parental control. We might say, somewhat tongue in cheek, that this moment arrives in conjunction with the child's possession of a driver's license. No authoritarian lines are long enough to keep parents in control of teenage drivers once they have backed a car out of the driveway. Instead, such moments begin to reveal to parents some important qualities in the young people they have been "authoring."

Novelists are another class of author—a word that derives from the same Latin root as the word "authority." They are, in one sense, authorities, if we consider a novelist's ability to create characters and weave them into plots that lead to endings either happy or sad. Many novelists say, however, that as their work develops, the characters in the story begin to take on a life of their own. Authors begin to discover that they no longer can make these fictional people say or do things that violate or otherwise contradict their fully developed characters. Authors find themselves engaged in a project that is very much a relationship, an interaction between themselves and the characters they have created. In a sense, the character "tells" the author what to write about him or her. For writers who experience this phenomenon, the authority of the author turns out to be creative and relational rather than dictatorial or authoritarian.[3]

It is in this sense of authority as "authoring" that we say the Bible is authoritative. Speaking for a moment as if the Bible were a person, we can say that the Bible's intention is to form men and women into the kind of people who can and will live faithfully as the people of the God who is the central actor of scripture. Theologian Stanley Hauerwas's statement serves to summarize this point: "The scripture functions as an authority for Christians precisely because by trying to live, think, and feel faithful to its witness they find they are more nearly able to live faithful to the truth. For the scripture forms a society [i.e., the church] and sets an agenda for its life that requires nothing less than trusting its existence to the God found through the stories of Israel and Jesus."[4]

The second point in Wickersham's definition follows on the first. *The Bible is authoritative in matters of theology and doctrine.* Before considering the arenas of biblical authority, it is important to say that in some areas the Bible is not authoritative. That may sound sacrilegious, or at least impious, but neither is our meaning or intent. We think, however, that Christians must not make claims for the Bible that it would not make for itself. For instance, the Bible does not claim to be history in the modern, conventional sense of that term. That is demonstrated by the difficulty of precisely dating biblical personalities and events solely on the basis of the biblical accounts. The Bible does not give us the years of King David's birth and death, for example, nor many other details that modern historians consider basic.

About what, then, *is* the Bible authoritative? The Bible speaks authoritatively about the most important matters in life—"meaning, life and death, with what things we fear and the persons we may trust, with relationships broken and restored, with the problems of guilt and how we may be forgiven."[5] The Bible speaks authoritatively of the God who works through history to make known his will for the whole of creation, the God who redeems, the God who creates, the God who restores. The Bible speaks authoritatively of the human situation. It teaches that humans are created beings and therefore less than God, and that human beings sin and therefore stand in need of forgiveness and redemption. The Bible speaks authoritatively of the ways in which humans can live in good relationships to each other and to the created order. The Bible speaks authoritatively about the mystery of life, death, and resurrection, and about the manner in which humans find meaning for life through their relationship with God. To say that the Bible is the church's theological and moral authority is to have said all this and more.

The third point to be made from Wickersham's statement on the inspiration and authority of the Bible is that *the Bible is authoritative and inspired*. When the topic of biblical inspiration comes up for discussion, many Christians think immediately of 2 Timothy 3:16–17—"All scripture is inspired by God and is useful for teaching, for reproof, for correction, and for training in righteousness, so that everyone who belongs to God may be proficient, equipped for every good work." Since at the time this epistle was written, the Christian church was still centuries away from agreement on a minimum list of canonical books of the Bible, we will set aside the important question of what the text might mean by "scripture." Instead we will ask another important question of this text: what does "inspired" mean?

H. C. Wickersham answered that question by saying, "The

different writers of the books of the Bible were inspired of God. It is not the words of the Bible that were inspired, it is not the thoughts of the Bible that were inspired; it is the men who wrote the Bible that were inspired. Inspiration acts not on the man's words, not on the man's thought, but on the man himself." The Greek word that we translate "inspired" is *theopneustos,* which literally means "God-breathed." Some Christians have interpreted this to mean that God dictated the very words of scripture. It seems clear enough that Wickersham did not share this view. Instead, he understood inspiration to be a divine activity that worked on the people of God who wrote those texts that later came to be gathered and authorized as the canonical scriptures. Inspiration, thought Wickersham, works on people, not things. Accordingly, the Bible is inspired as it is a result of God's action among men and women of the inspired community, the people of God.

Wickersham's account of the Bible as the work of inspired people also introduces the question of the church's role in the biblical interpretation. Much traditional teaching on this subject has insisted that the church should interpret scripture for individual Christians. Others have argued that neither church body nor creed should impose its doctrine on individuals, to whom must be reserved the right of private interpretation. The early Church of God minister and writer D. Otis Teasley thought that both perspectives mistakenly viewed the relation between scripture, the individual reader, and the church. "A more useful approach to this question would result," said Teasley, "in a respectful balance between the community and the individual: 'The church is not given the supreme right to interpret the Bible for the individual, nor is the individual given the right regardless of unity and peace to interpret the

Bible contrary to the general belief of the true church and force his belief upon others.' "[6] The interpretation of scripture, in other words, is a three-cornered "conversation" between the Bible, the church, and individual believers. Take away any one element and interpretive problems are certain to arise.

1.3 Implications for Teaching

When we think of biblical teaching and interpretation in this manner we begin to see the role and responsibility of the Bible teacher, whether in pulpit or church school classroom. In the all-important work of interpreting the Bible, the Bible teacher stands in the position of "church" in the three-cornered conversation. The teacher is an enabler of this conversation.

Effective teachers will work to bring together the voice of scripture, the voice of the church, and the voices of their class members as they work at the task of applying the insights of the Bible to the challenges of everyday life. As these voices speak to each other in the church school classroom, the relations basic to Christian discipleship will be nourished. The teacher's role, then, embraces much more than that of an authoritative voice of church doctrine, although it will benefit all if the teacher has a basic knowledge of church teaching. It is not, however, the teacher's responsibility to indoctrinate the class; that would be equivalent to the church imposing its doctrinal tradition on individuals, in effect telling them the text's meaning. Nor can the teacher merely sit back and listen as class members create their own imaginative interpretations. Instead, the Bible teacher acts as the facilitator for a great conversation as the church of the past (doctrinal tradition) and the church of the present (the Sunday school class) come together to interpret scripture for the mutual encouragement and strengthening of Christ's disciples.

For Christians who, like those in the Church of God movement, resist the normative teaching authority of the creeds, there is an important further point. In the absence of authoritative creeds to enforce a kind of doctrinal uniformity, serious Bible study will include an attitude of respectful attention to each voice in the study group or class. None of us will ever master the Bible and its interpretation. Each of us reads the scripture from the unique perspective of our own life setting. Therefore it seems only reasonable that careful study and interpretation of the Bible will give attention to the perspectives of all, since each perspective carries the potential of opening up the biblical text to a meaning that others who do not share that perspective cannot see.

The church is an extended conversation about the implications for Christian discipleship of the stories of God, Israel, Jesus and the church. To be better able to answer the question, "What kind of people is God calling us to be?" is one important motive for our attendance at church school and worship where we are engaged by the Bible and enter into conversation with the saints of the present and past.

As we answer this question and determine to live according to its answers, we grow as disciples. Our transformation into disciples of the Lord Jesus Christ is therefore one crucial consequence of our participation in worship and the church's educational ministries. Thus the role of the Bible teacher is to assist fellow Christians as they grow by God's grace in this transforming work. Teachers fulfill this role—a calling—when they create a classroom climate that enables people to be grounded in and formed by the great narrative of the Bible, that is, the story[7] of the God who searches for and calls a people to be God's own and live faithfully to God for the sake of the world's redemption.

Notes

1. Wickersham, 1894, 18–19.
2. Brueggemann, 1968, 2.
3. For a further discussion of the various ideas of authority, see "Managers and Sages: The Idea of Authority and the Church of God Movement" in Merle D. Strege, *Tell Me Another Tale: Historical Reflections on the Church of God,* (Anderson, Ind: Warner Press, 1993), 119–135.
4. Hauerwas, 1981, 66.
5. Brueggemann, 3–4.
6. Strege, 1993, 165–166.
7. By "story" we have something in mind far more significant than an entertaining diversion or cute means of holding people's attention. Neither do we have in mind the idea of a fiction. Rather, we use the term "story" because the Bible's primary form of talking about God is story. Indeed, we agree with Stanley Hauerwas, who asserts that there is no more fundamental way to talk about God than by means of story. From Genesis to Revelation, with some important exceptions along the way to be sure, the vast majority of biblical literature is narrative in structure and style. The Bible describes a God who acts; when God acts things happen, and when things happen you have a story with a beginning, a middle, and an ending. Christians, of course, are people who commit their whole lives to the truthfulness of the God who is the main actor in the biblical narratives.

Chapter Two

God*

—Merle Strege—

To the King of the ages, immortal, invisible, the
only God, be honor and glory forever and ever ...
—he who is the blessed and only Sovereign,
the King of kings and Lord of lords. It is he
alone who has immortality and dwells in
unapproachable light, whom no one has ever
seen or can see; to him be honor and eternal dominion.
Amen.
—1 Timothy 1:17 & 6:15–16 (NRSV)

2.0 God and the Bible

The Bible speaks of God in remarkably straightforward
language, using concrete terms and expressions. The Bible
does not speculate about God. It does not engage in philosophical arguments to demonstrate God's existence. Neither
does it speculate about God's nature or speak of God in
abstract language. The Bible begins with the simple, direct
assumption—God exists; no argument or demonstration is
necessary.

*Walter Brueggemann's brilliant exposition of this topic in *Hope Within
History,* 58–69, is the source of these ideas. All of section 2.4 is deeply indebted
to his analysis.

God is the subject of the Bible, not the object of detached observation and discussion. God is the protagonist or "hero" who initiates action. The Bible's very first sentence places God at the center of this unfolding story: "In the beginning when God created the heavens and the earth ..." (Gen 1:1). God creates. With this action verb history begins. The Bible's next-to-last verse petitions the Lord to act again, in this case to bring history to a close: "Amen. Come, Lord Jesus!" (Rev 22:20). In scripture God is the agent who sets history into motion and the agent who acts in history to work the divine will. This is one meaning of the claim that God is the subject of the Bible.

There is another meaning to this claim. The Bible speaks in God's voice. It discloses the very mind and intention of God, so in this sense God is also the implied narrator of the biblical story. God is the subject within the story, the subject behind the story, and the author of the story.

A dominant theme running throughout scripture is that we are to pay attention to what people do; Jesus said that we would know who people are by their "fruit." The Bible's primary way of speaking about God is in the action-oriented language of narrative. Narrative means story. Narrative language means that the Bible tells stories using a language appropriate to storytelling. It does this on purpose. God makes things happen, and there is no more basic way to describe events than in the form of a story. Given the Bible's narrative language, we read much about what God does. God creates. God judges. God redeems. God delivers. God chastises. God comforts. God heals. God saves. In the Bible we are introduced to God's character or nature primarily through stories that inform us about what God has done. As we learn what God has done, we are able to make theological statements about the kind of God it is who has done such deeds. We know who God is by God's "fruit."

The Bible's purpose, of course, is far greater than simply reporting God's activities. The Bible tells us of God for reasons beyond providing material for philosophical and theological discussions about God's nature. If God is the subject of the Bible, then surely scripture shares with God the divine purpose of salvation for all. Rightly grasped, the Bible intends to form a people morally and spiritually that they might live in faithful relationship to the God who is its subject. Old Testament writings often exhort Israel to "turn" from their sin to Yahweh. The New Testament exhorts people similarly to "repent," to make an about-face, a 180 degree turn from a life without God and hope to the life of salvation. The Bible tells the story of God because—if we are to be saved—we must know who this God is and the shape of the life expected of the people of God.

One helpful way to think of the gracious forgiveness of God (which is our salvation) and the changes that grow out of our new state (which is our continuing conversion) is to see such change as the result of a collision of stories. Each of us is the personal story of our own life. We were born to a set of parents at a particular place and time; we have made various choices down to the very present; and we have certain specific values and goals for our life. At some point during our personal story, we come to the Bible and learn of God. This is not just any God, but Yahweh who called Israel out of bondage, who gave Israel land and blessing, who sought Israel when the people wandered away from Yahweh's will, who sent Jesus as Israel's Messiah and the now opened door of salvation for the Gentiles, and who inspires the church to be the agent of God's ongoing activity in the world.

Then, the great narrative of God and the narrative of our own life cross paths. In repentance we learn to see our own life not only on its own terms but also reinterpreted through the story of God. We come to interpret the very meaning of our existence as bound up with the life of God as revealed to us through the pages of the Bible. In other words, we read the biblical story of God for much the same reason that Peter gave Jesus when asked why he and the other disciples did not also leave the Master: "Lord, to whom can we go? You have the words of eternal life" (John 6:68). Thus, this book begins and ends with the God whose word and deeds lead to life.

2.1 God and Redemption

While the Bible begins in Genesis with the creation of the world, the Old Testament story more accurately begins with the Exodus. Israel first understood God as the redeemer who freed Israel from its life of oppression and its status as a non-people (see Hos 2:23 and 1 Pet 2:10). Pharaoh's ragtag, Israelite slaves were little more than a rabble, a non-nation without an identity. Yahweh liberated this nonpeople in the Exodus, redeeming them from the house of bondage and freeing them for life together in covenant relationship with him. Thus God commands Moses to say to the Israelites, "I will redeem you with an outstretched arm and with mighty acts of judgment. I will take you as my people, and I will be your God" (Exod 6:6b–7). In Deuteronomy, one of God's distinctive qualities that the Israelites are commanded to remember is that God is redeemer, the one who "brought you [Israel] out of the land of Egypt and redeemed you from the house of slavery" (Deut 13:5).

God's character as redeemer extended far beyond the people's memory of the redeeming act of the Exodus. Throughout the Old Testament's narratives and praises to God, Yahweh's character as Israel's redeemer tints the text. The Genesis account of creation connects Yahweh—God of Abraham, Isaac, and Jacob, God of the Exodus—with the origin of creation. The Genesis narrative "asserts that Yahweh is still God, one who watches over his creation and will bring it to well-being."[1] In the Genesis account of Israel's claim that the redeemer God is also the creator God, the Old Testament is not simply offering an account of the origins of the universe. Rather, its unfolding narrative of the creation makes the bold theological claim that the God of creation is the God of Israel.

Israel's perception of Yahweh as redeemer is not limited to a one-time experience in Egypt. Thus the psalmist prayed, "Redeem Israel, O God, out of all its troubles" (Ps 25:22). Israel's practice of calling on Yahweh in time of trouble rests on this fundamental conception of God as the one who redeems Israel. Walter Brueggemann describes this practice as the "cry-save" motif that undergirded the early Israelite covenant community of the judges and Samuel. Commenting on Israel's reply to the Philistine threat in 1 Samuel 7:5–11, Brueggemann says, "In its petition to Samuel, Israel uses the most elemental terms of Israel's faith, 'cry, save,' 'You cry that Yahweh may save' (v 8). Samuel is responsive; he does cry out to Yahweh on behalf of Israel. As promised in verse 3, Yahweh hears, answers and acts. The Philistines are defeated. Israel is delivered [we might say that Israel has been redeemed]. Samuel is vindicated. Yahweh is known to be faithful to Israel. Covenantal modes of faith and power do indeed operate."[2]

Devastating calamities befell Israel in the eighth through

the sixth centuries bc. First the Assyrians and next the Babylonians invaded the Divided Monarchies of Israel and Judah. The great prophets, nevertheless, held firm to the faith that Yahweh would again redeem Israel. Thus Isaiah 43:1 encourages Israel against fear, "for I have redeemed you, I have called you by name."

The prophet Jeremiah perceived that the armies of Nebuchadnezzar would force Israel to pass through fire and sword to eat the dry, tasteless, bread of exile. But there would also come a day of redemption, as Yahweh promised, "For I am with you to save you and deliver you, says the Lord. I will deliver you out of the hand of the wicked and redeem you from the grasp of the ruthless" (Jer 15:20b–21).

Both Isaiah and Jeremiah hold out to Israel Yahweh's promised redemption from exile. Furthermore, and especially in the Book of Isaiah, we find Yahweh's pledge of Israel's redemption through the agency of the promised Messiah. Whether remembering Yahweh's action in the Exodus, crying out to Yahweh for protection from marauding Philistines, or looking to a future restoration after the purging experience of exile, Israel characteristically thought of God as the redeemer.

2.11 God's Redemption, Covenant, and Obedience

One side of Israelite thought interpreted Yahweh's character as redeemer so as to conclude that God would never break the covenant made with Israel through Moses. In this view God's covenant with Israel is absolute. There is no real choice: Yahweh must act to redeem Israel for the sake of the covenant made with Abraham and Moses. God had graciously covenanted with Abraham that he would be given descendants and land. Moreover, God promised to keep covenant with Abraham's descendants as well. Thus says Yahweh to Abraham, "I will establish my covenant between me and you, and your offspring after you throughout their generations, for an everlasting covenant, to be God to you and to your offspring after you. And I will give to you, and to your offspring after you, the land where you are now an alien, all the land of Canaan, for a perpetual holding; and I will be their God" (Gen 17:7–8).

Another interpretation of Yahweh the redeemer emerged centuries later, after the years of bondage in Egypt and the Exodus, after the return to Canaan and the establishment of the monarchy under Saul and David. At this time many Israelites understood Yahweh's covenant with Abraham to apply in a specialized way to Jerusalem and the monarchy enthroned there. "This rather different notion of covenant had in the national mind largely superseded that of the primitive covenant [with Abraham and Moses]. It was believed and affirmed in Israelite forms of worship that Yahweh had chosen Zion as his dwelling and promised to David an eternal dynasty; that each king, as Yahweh's anointed 'son' (Ps 2:7), would be protected from his foes; that the dynasty would in the end gain a domain greater than David's, with the kings of the earth fawning at its feet (Ps 2:10f.; 72:8–11; etc.).

Judah's existence, in short, did not rest on obedient response to the gracious acts of Yahweh in the past, but in his unconditional promises for the future."[3] This confidence in Yahweh's everlasting covenant with Israel through the Davidic monarchy has been variously labeled the "Jerusalem," "royal," or "official" theology. These terms all refer to the same attitude and interpretation of Yahweh's role as Israel's redeemer. It was an interpretation that concluded

35

that, for the sake of his covenant with David, Yahweh would always protect and redeem the nation.

Alongside the Abrahamic covenant and the official or royal theology of covenant, one also finds in Israel a third and very different interpretation of Yahweh as redeemer. In this view Yahweh will act on behalf of Israel if, and only if, the people walk faithfully with Yahweh according to the instruction of Torah. This interpretation of the covenant gives Yahweh's role as redeemer a broad freedom unknown in the royal theology. Yahweh will redeem, but in ways that may surprise Israel. In this view Yahweh's continuing favor rests on Israelite obedience to the ethical commandments of Torah. The classical expression of this interpretation of the covenant is 2 Chronicles 7:13–14: "When I shut up the heavens so that there is no rain, or command the locust to devour the land, or send pestilence among my people, if my people who are called by my name humble themselves, pray, seek my face, and turn from their wicked ways, then will I hear from heaven, and will forgive their sin and heal their land." Through to the conclusion of 2 Chronicles 7, the text elaborates Yahweh's promise of redemption and blessing, one that depends on Israel's obedience to the covenant.

No religious movement or force within Israelite history articulated the contingent or relational nature of Yahweh's character as redeemer with greater force or clarity than the great prophets beginning in the eighth century BC and culminating in the magnificent preaching of Isaiah and Jeremiah. According to the traditional explanation of the role of prophecy in Israel, "the prophets were therefore in the first place custodians and traditioners of Torah," the law given to Moses and the consequence of Yahweh's covenant with him. "Prophetic indictments often follow quite closely stipulations of law in the Pentateuch, and verdicts of divine judgement pronounced by prophets often correspond to curses attached to laws."[4] The prophets' judgments against Israel were rooted in the national failure to live according to the covenant between Yahweh and Moses, the very core of which was Torah. Such failure meant that Israel could not rely on Yahweh's continued protection against foreign domination. The people had violated the conditions of their covenant with Yahweh, and such transgression, thundered the prophets, would cost Israel dearly.

Isaiah 5, the "Song of the Vineyard," illustrates the prophetic insistence that the nation follow the Mosaic covenant or suffer the consequences:

> For the vineyard of the LORD of hosts
>   is the house of Israel,
> and the people of Judah
>   are his pleasant planting;
> he expected justice,
>   but saw bloodshed;
> righteousness,
>   but heard a cry!
> Ah you who join house to house,
>   who add field to field,
> until there is room for no one but you,
>   and you are left to live alone
> in the midst of the land!
> The LORD of hosts has sworn in
>   my hearing:
> Surely many houses shall be
>   desolate,
> large and beautiful houses,
>   without inhabitant.
>
> (Isaiah 5:7–9)

2.12 The prophetic word of Isaiah

Isaiah lived during the years when the northern kingdom of Israel collapsed in the face of Assyrian aggression. Even though his own land, the southern kingdom of Judah, experienced great prosperity, Isaiah grew increasingly uneasy with the tendency of Judah's King Ahaz to trust in international political alliances more than in Yahweh's power to save Israel. Isaiah's attitude toward the pragmatic politics of alliances and diplomacy reminds one of Samuel's deep distrust of monarchy as an institution that could secure Israel. The elders of the nation insisted that Samuel give them a king "like the nations." Samuel resisted the request until God finally told him to grant it, saying that it was not Samuel but Yahweh that the people rejected. Similarly, Isaiah charged Judah's leaders with a lack of faith and covenant loyalty to Yahweh, preferring to trust in their own political skills. They trusted in human arrangements and institutions more than they trusted Yahweh's power to save.

Isaiah leveled a second indictment against Judah. In this case he charged the nation for failing to do justice. As the prophet laments in the Song of the Vineyard, God established the Israelites in the land of Canaan and expected them to live according to the ethical requirements of the covenant. Yahweh saw bloodshed, however, where he had expected to find justice and heard the cry of oppression in place of the song of righteousness. "But the Lord of hosts is exalted by justice, and the Holy God shows himself holy by righteousness" (Isa 5:16). Not only could Israel expect to lose Yahweh's saving, redeeming action on its behalf; for the want of justice in the land, Judah could also now look forward to divine punishment.

2.13 The prophetic word of Jeremiah

Perhaps more than any other prophet, Jeremiah saw God's redemption of Israel at work in the punishment for its transgressions of covenant morality. Only the prophet Hosea comes close to Jeremiah's understanding of Yahweh's redemptive purposes through suffering—an ache and a suffering that afflicts even God's heart. Jeremiah's call to be a prophet came during the reign of King Josiah, but he first challenged public authorities during the reign of King Johoiakim (609—598 BC). In sermons that could be interpreted only as unpatriotic in Judah, Jeremiah told his listeners that the king of Babylon soon would enter Jerusalem and destroy the nation. Unrighteousness and disobedience to Yahweh's covenant continued throughout the land, especially in the high circles of government and religious leadership. The nation had failed to keep the conditions of God's covenant, and, said Jeremiah, Yahweh had determined to punish the people. Why is it that God will not destroy Israel completely?

> The presumed world in Jerusalem is one of strict retribution, and the proposed world of Jeremiah is that God still wills a relationship, in spite of the failure of Jerusalem. There is an ache in God's heart, the ache of fidelity, the ache yearning to continue to be faithful, even in the face of rejection.... This ache in God's heart is more painful and more difficult and more passionate than what people hear when we use the word grace. From time to time in Jeremiah, what happens is that the power of God's ache overrides the relentless if.[6]

Jeremiah perceived that God's judgment was not simply vengeful, with no purpose greater than punishment. Instead, Jeremiah saw that Israel's punishment served the larger purposes of Yahweh's desire to redeem the people. God remained the redeemer, but Jeremiah understood that Yahweh's redemption of Israel would be accomplished as suffering and exile chastised the people of Judah. Speaking for the Lord, Jeremiah proclaimed: "In this place of which you say, 'It is a waste without human beings or animals,' in the towns of Judah and the streets of Jerusalem that are desolate, without inhabitants, human or animal, there shall once more be heard the voice of mirth and the voice of gladness, the voice of the bridegroom and the voice of the bride, the voices of those who sing, as they bring thank offerings to the house of the Lord:

> "Give thanks to the LORD of hosts,
>   for the LORD is good,
>   for his steadfast love endures forever!"
> For I will restore the fortunes of the land as at first,
> says the LORD.
>
> (Jeremiah 33:11)

On the other side of Israelite suffering, then, beams the hope of restoration and redemption. Even in the Israelite experience of exile Yahweh remains the redeemer. After the decadence and injustice of the divided monarchies, Israel will come to new insight on God's redemption.

The prophet Jeremiah looks into God's heart, as it were, and gives us a profoundly paradoxical vision of Yahweh. First Jeremiah shows us Yahweh the redeemer who enters into covenant with Israel and insists that if the nation obeys the commandments all will be well. Second Jeremiah shows us Yahweh the redeemer who carries deep within his heart the ache of unrequited love, for the sake of which he will not let Israel go. Jeremiah's perception of God is very much like Jesus' picture of the waiting father who endures the faithless slights of a rebellious son only to sit patiently by the window, hoping for his return. The conditional if will not be imposed; only let the son return. So it is with Yahweh, the redeemer God of Israel's covenant.

2.2 God Hears the Cry of the Sufferer

Israel, and thus the Old Testament, articulates its experience of Yahweh as redeemer out of its distinctive belief that Yahweh hears the cry of pain. This belief was peculiar to Israel. More typically the gods of the ancient world were shaped by rich, powerful and privileged people in ways that benefited them; their gods rewarded the behavior of those who shared the values of the rich and powerful. In other words, the gods of the ancient world sanctioned the established order, thereby endorsing the social power of "the best sort of people" and the social status quo.

One does find this concept in the Old Testament in the attitude that God blesses the righteous and punishes the wicked—an idea readily found in the theologies and mythologies of Israel's neighbors. But this important biblical idea is easily corrupted into the belief that prosperity, power, and privilege are unquestionable signs of God's blessing—a common theology, then and now.

The Bible and the God of the Bible refuse, however, to be forced into a simplistic, one-sided, position on this point. Job's friends set forth the claim that prosperity clearly

41

demonstrates God's favor, and they also articulate its negative side—"Know then that God exacts of you less than your guilt deserves" (Job 11:6). Yet, virtually the entire Book of Job stands as a criticism of this position. The Old Testament includes Job's critical voice because Israel had learned that God heard and answered its cry of pain. Far from closing his ear to the oppressed and the silent sufferer, God is the one who hears the cry of pain, especially the pain of injustice. Yahweh even hears the voice of the murderer's dead victim: "And the Lord said [to Cain], 'What have you done? Listen; your brother's blood is crying out to me from the ground!' " (Gen 4:10). Yahweh's character as Israel's redeemer rises out of his capacity to hear Israel's cry against the injustice of its miserable life in Egypt.

Old Testament people believed that Yahweh embraced the pain of those who cried out to him.

> By *embrace of pain* is meant the full acknowledgment of pain and the capacity and willingness to make that pain a substantive part of Israel's faith conversation with its God. Such an act of embrace means to articulate the pain fully, to insist on God's reception of the speech and the pain, and to wait hopefully for God's resolution. The term 'pain' here refers to any dysfunction in the relationship with God and to any derivative dysfunction in the disorder of creation or society. The pain may be experienced in quite public or private ways. But it is all of a piece, because such acknowledgement and articulation are an assertion that the modes of common theology are not adequate ... to this experience.[7]

Unlike the gods of its neighbors, Israel's God was not limited to managing the natural processes of creation as rainfall, drought, and the change of seasons. Nor was the role of

Israel's God narrowly expressed through the established social and political orders and rituals of temple and monarchy. Yahweh's domain spanned more than creation and the cultural order. Above both the natural and cultural worlds, Yahweh heard the cry of pain that protested when matters were not as they should be. This bold cry even dared ask of God, "Shall not the Judge of the all the earth do what is just?" (Gen 18:25).

Yahweh's character as Israel's redeemer, and thus the great biblical theme of redemption, begins in the divine capacity to hear and embrace people's cries of pain. Thus Yahweh says to Moses, "I have observed the misery of my people who are in Egypt; I have heard their cry on account of their taskmasters" (Exod 3:7).

Thus Hannah, her cry to Yahweh heard, sang: "The bows of the mighty are broken, / but the feeble gird on strength. Those who were full have hired themselves out for bread, / but those who were hungry are fat with spoil.... The Lord makes poor and makes rich; / he brings low, he also exalts. He raises up the poor from the dust; / he lifts the needy from the ash heap, / to make them sit with princes and inherit a seat of honor" (1 Sam 2:4–5, 7–8).

Thus in the face of overwhelming disaster, Job insists: "For I know that my Redeemer lives, / and that at last he will stand upon the earth; / and after my skin has been thus destroyed, then in my flesh I shall see God, / whom I shall see on my side, / and my eyes shall behold, and not another" (Job 19:25–27).

Thus declared Isaiah, "The people who walked in darkness / have seen a great light; / those who lived in a land of deep darkness— / on them light has shined. / You have multiplied the nation, / you have increased its joy; / they rejoice before

43

you as with joy at the harvest, / as people exult when dividing plunder. / For the yoke of their burden, / and the bar across their shoulders, / the rod of their oppressor, / you have broken as on the day of Midian" (Isa 9:2–4).

Thus sang Mary, "My soul magnifies the Lord, / and my spirit rejoices in God my Savior, / for he has looked with favor on the lowliness of his servant ... / He has shown strength with his arm; / he has scattered the proud in the thoughts of their hearts. / He has brought down the powerful from their thrones, / and lifted up the lowly; / he has filled the hungry with good things, / and sent the rich away empty. / He has helped his servant Israel, / in remembrance of his mercy, / according to the promise he made to our ancestors, / to Abraham and to his descendants forever" (Luke 1:46–48, 51–55).

2.3 God the Redeemer and Life in its Setting

2.31 The Temptation to Insulate Ourselves against Pain

It is an old and accurate observation that human beings will usually seek pleasure and avoid pain. In many ways this is perfectly normal. Most of us prefer comfort to discomfort, satisfied stomachs to hunger pangs, a comfortable sofa over a metal folding chair. Psychologically healthy people avoid pain and seek pleasure, and the behavior of those who intentionally seek pain raises questions about their mental health. It is also, however, possible to avoid pain and harm ourselves in the process. Physical exercise is an important component of a person's health and often may be accompanied by some degree of discomfort or pain—aching muscles, stiffness, or soreness. Avoiding these discomforts can prove harmful to a person's health. Masking pain, covering it with pain-relievers, can also prove harmful. In medical terms, pain is a symptom. Something causes pain in our bodies, and we should not ignore that pain or mask it without knowing its cause. Burning stomachs can be the result of too many french fries—or an ulcer. Pain is one way that our bodies signal us that things are not as they should be. Wise people will attempt to discover the cause of pain.

What do our ways of dealing with pain have to do with the Bible and the God who is its central actor? Our lives often are touched by kinds of pain that aspirin cannot relieve. People suffer the pain of separation, alienation, and loneliness—even in the midst of great crowds. The circle of human pain enlarges dramatically if we include unhappiness as a kind of pain. People suffer the unhappy pain that accompanies failures, whether vocational, financial, educational, or domestic. One of the deepest pains we can suffer originates in failed hopes or expectations. We suffer deeply when the hopes of a new job or school year or relationship go awry. Even the creation suffers the pain of disappointed hope. Thus the Bible says, "The creation was subjected to futility, not of its own will but by the will of the one who subjected it, in hope that the creation itself will be set free from its bondage to decay and will obtain the freedom of the glory of the children of God. We know that the whole creation has been groaning in labor pains until now" (Rom 8:20–22).

In the Ten Commandments the Bible addresses some of the root causes of human hurt. We often inflict pain on ourselves, as when we break the first commandment and refuse to allow God to be lord of our lives. The later commandments warn us against further self-inflicted pain, as when we subject ourselves to the gnawing hurts of envy and covetousness. These

45

lead to a restless acquisitiveness that pains us doubly; we are seduced into the false belief that material goods yield security. Then in pursuit of this false security we come to refuse one day's rest in seven.

Not all pain is self-inflicted. To suffer injustice is to experience a deep-seated pain at the hands of others. Israel's awareness and experience of Yahweh as redeemer began in the unrelieved misery of oppression visited upon them by slave-masters in Egypt. The other-inflicted pain of injustice may very well be the other side of the coin of the self-inflicted pain of acquisitiveness. It only stands to reason that some have too little because others have too much. To have either too much or too little will prove to hurt someone. The Bible speaks very clearly about this double-sided, pain-producing problem and dares to imagine a social reality where every need is supplied, but not every want.

We find ourselves afflicted and surrounded by pain. Because humans naturally seek pleasure and avoid pain, we will go to elaborate lengths to insulate ourselves against it. Just as we take pain-relievers to relieve ourselves of headache, so we attempt to treat the symptoms of the pain of sin, loneliness, and despair without attending to their causes. Today one hears the phrase "deferred gratification" spoken with a certain wistfulness, as if nobody believes or practices that anymore. To defer gratification means to endure deprivation and pain, if only temporarily, in order to realize some future goal.

For example, today many Americans believe that people may freely choose to engage in sexual intercourse with or without benefit of marriage. The assumption is that human beings have sexual needs that should be met; gratification of the need takes priority over other concerns. Over against the society's general belief, the church lifts up the ideal of celibacy or virginity until marriage, despite the powerful sexual urges racing through adolescent bodies. Nevertheless, much of our society views this stance as if it were little more than a charming relic from the Victorian past. Pleasure, believes society, need not be deferred, for to defer pleasure may increase pain.

These reflections on one American social tendency point up the contrast between our modern American world and the world of the Bible. One could illustrate additional examples of this tendency, for instance our ready willingness to spend vast sums of money for over-the-counter and prescription drugs in the pursuit of relief from pain and discomfort. This is not to suggest that people should seek pain, but to point out this tendency in society because it stands in stark contrast to the Bible's depiction of God's way of dealing with human hurt.

The God of the Bible resists human efforts to escape or mask pain. God stands ready to redeem the world's pain. The God of the Bible redeems our suffering and the world's suffering by embracing it, which is to say that God hears and responds to those who cry out in pain. God takes their hurt into his own life and redeems it.

This redemption begins in God's gracious willingness to embrace our and the world's pain, but God hears our cry only if we cry. If we do not cry, if we try to mask our pain through self-management or precise theological formulas, we shut ourselves off from the One who stands ready to anoint us with the balm of Gilead. Our refusal to embrace our own pain and the pain of the world's suffering closes us off from the possibility that God will hear our cry. With our own resources we may treat the symptoms, perhaps even successfully mask

47

them. We will not find healing; that, alone, is the province of God the redeemer.

2.32 God, Pain, Redemption, and Hope

If pain is a symptom meant to warn us that things are not as they should be, and if God embraces pain for the sake of redeeming its cause, then we may conclude that God desires restoration and wholeness. God heard Israel's cry in Egypt and sent Moses to deliver the people from bondage. God heard Hannah's cry for a son and Samuel was born. God heard Job's cry for an answer to the riddle of a life devastated by evil, and the Lord answered him out of the whirlwind. Psalm 51 records David's penitent cry that his sin be forgiven, and the Lord restored him.

The Israelite exiles in Babylon cried out to God for release from their captivity and Yahweh delivered them through his servant Cyrus. The very act of crying out to the Lord already counterbalances the sufferer's desperate situation. People who persistently cry out to God make poor subjects or victims. Slaves cry out and hope to be liberated; a childless woman cries to God and simultaneously dares to hope that barrenness will give way to motherhood; a sinner cries out for forgiveness and in that very act hopes for restoration. God hears such cries; therefore, our situation is not hopeless. Our suffering and the situation that produces it will not last forever.

There are those, on the other hand, who benefit from situations that produce suffering and pain for others. Clearly the Egyptians benefited from Israelite forced labor, as did the Babylonians and the Assyrians hundreds of years later. Peninah benefited from Hannah's barrenness, the former enjoying her status of the more favored of Elkanah's wives. It is in the interest of such individuals and groups to keep the status quo intact. To maintain the stability, they will attempt to mute the cry of pain that threatens to destabilize the situation that benefits them. They create institutions of social stability, and these spawn attitudes that rob persons of their voice and ultimately their hope. The absence of hope leads to despair, and most know its voice all too well: "It's no use." "You can't change the system." "Things will never change." Against these voices of hopelessness, God the redeemer stands ready to enter the situation and transform it.

Social institutions serve stability. Humans have government, law, education, and religion to order and preserve our life together. For instance, learning and teaching are possible apart from schools and universities, but these institutions preserve and facilitate the practices that combine to encourage learning. In the very process of preserving such valuable activities, social institutions may actually mask or mute people's frustration and pain. Intentional or not, to silence another's cry without attending to its source is to resist the process of history-making in which God is engaged. God makes history as situations of pain are redeemed. History-making people are aligned with God's redemptive purposes. We tend to think that history is made by the famous, the great, and the powerful; however, over and over through the pages of the Bible we see God at work, making history through the lives of people who are passed over unnoticed by the great and the powerful.

"The history-making process in ancient Israel is done through the voice of marginality which is spoken by prophetic figures and those with whom they make common cause."[8] The marginal peoples of scripture and the world are those who live on the ragged edges of society. They lack power and often are oppressed. The prophets' role as history-makers, articulating the cry of the farmers and shepherds, the little people who suffered injustice at the hands of the royal bureaucracy and the special interests of the Jerusalem establishment, comes to clear focus in the judgment they delivered against the powerful and privileged.

Walter Brueggemann interprets the tension between Israel's kings and its prophets as the product of Yahweh's way of making history through the voices and cries of marginal people. Kings, whether Israelite or other, have an interest in social order and stability. They are not very interested in large-scale change. They use their power to control communication and to keep the lid on change. They protect the vested interests of the movers and shakers in their society. The king who is attentive to the cries of suffering thereby acknowledges that something is wrong. Something in the society needs change.

Such an acknowledgment thus threatens to destabilize the social order. Israel's great prophets break into the royal system and the upper levels of Israelite society from the outside. The prophets come to the palace from its margins and challenge the monarchy at the point of its moral and theological failings. But the prophets also challenge the monarchy for its efforts to ignore the cries of people who are suffering injustice and oppression. Kings who try to manage society according to the desires of the great and powerful inevitably run afoul of the history-making power of Yahweh. Prophecy in Israel served to open up Israelite religious, ethical, social, and political life, but from the royal point of view, prophecy—what Yahweh was doing in Israel—was a destabilizing factor.[9]

Brueggemann explains how hope arises out of suffering

and prevents that cry from collapsing into despair. He contends that hope forces us to consider present arrangements of social power as open-ended; they can be changed as long as hope is present. As long as people are hopeful, "the way things are" is unstable. As Brueggemann says, "Hope reminds us not to take [the present situation] too seriously, not to treat it too honorably, because it will not last."[10] Yahweh's capacity to hear Israel's cry of suffering enabled marginalized people to hope in Yahweh. This hope gave them a vantage point from which to critically examine and even judge the social system of which they were part. Such critical examination allows people to believe that things can be changed. Hopeless people fall into a despair that leads inevitably to conformity. But hopeful people will not readily bend their necks to the yoke of oppression or even the status quo. Hope serves to remind us that all social arrangements are finite and limited; none of them grasps Yahweh's truth. Their claims to a completeness that they cannot ever possess are in reality expressions of idolatry.

The tense relationship between Israel's kings and prophets illustrates the power of marginalized hope's critical vantage point outside the royal system. Israel's kings always had to contend with prophets who forced them to face their shortcomings. Saul has his Samuel. Ahab has his Elijah. Jehoiakim, Jehoichin, and Zedekiah must face Jeremiah. Even David, the "man after God's own heart," is confronted by Nathan. A prophet is always around to remind the king of his proper business in the sight of God. It is that perspective that provides the vantage point outside the dominant royal culture. Israelite kings always stand under divine judgment and that judgment refuses to allow them to define their role and their society according to their own terms. Hurt and suffering people on the margins of an Israelite society crafted by kings can call out to the God who holds kings in check. As long as people have hope in the power of that cry and the God who hears it, they will not utterly depend on the "system"; they will not be easily governed by administrators from the royal bureaucracy. By their very presence and their hope, such people leave present social arrangements in a precarious state.

2.4 God's History-makers

History-makers are those who will not allow their present situation to push them into despair. They refuse to allow institutions and persons interested in maintaining the status quo to numb the reality of pain and the awareness that things are not as they should be. One need not possess power or privilege to be a history-maker. Indeed, the Bible is full of examples of everyday people who turn out to be history-makers because they cried out to God who heard their cry and redeemed the situation that was so hurtful to them. Their cry invited God into historical situations that were radically altered by God's power of redemption. This is what it means to be a history-maker. "There is no doubt that the Bible narrates a genuine history of humanity with the reality of pain and amazement, of death and life. There is no doubt also that the Bible narrates the powerful hope-filled promises of God which seem to operate and be visible in the processes of historical interaction."[11]

What are the characteristics of people who are history-makers? Walter Brueggemann proposes that the prophet Jeremiah provides a model for history-makers and offers five distinguishing marks:

2.41 "A Profound and Personal Sense of Anguish, Pathos, and Incongruity"

The prophet experiences anguish, that is, the pain of body or mind that results in distress. It is a personal anguish. The prophet senses that life is not as God meant it to be, that there is a lack of harmony, and that "time is out of joint."

The prophet is one in whom the standard, everyday occurrences of injustice and injury produce shrieks of rage and anger. A person who reads the prophets encounters speeches about widows, orphans, and the corruption of government and business. "They make much ado about paltry things, lavishing excessive language upon trifling subjects. What if somewhere in ancient Palestine poor people have not been treated properly by the rich?... Why such immoderate excitement? Why such intense indignation? The things that horrified the prophets are even now daily occurrences all over the world. There is no society to which Amos' words would not apply."[12] Biblical religion identifies with the hurt, the sorrow, and the rage of people who cannot find justice and see no merciful face turned toward them. No offense is too small, no person is so insignificant that this hurt is unimportant. Pain matters to God. That greed and corruption reign in the world of politics and business matters to God. Abuse and victimization matter to God. When systems and bureaucracies turn a deaf ear, God hears.

2.42 "Confidence in the Moral Coherence of the World"

The prophets understand and believe that the created world is a moral world that is connected and harmonious. Actions have consequences—often beyond our capacity to predict.

Job's great affirmation, "I know that my Redeemer lives, and that at the last he will stand upon the earth," is fundamentally a statement of confidence that the world is morally coherent. People who complain that the wicked prosper while good people suffer affirm by that very protest that such situations do not represent the world as originally intended. Evil and devious people may escape the consequences of their sins for a season, but God and the moral coherence of God's creation will not be flouted forever. Many Americans are learning in the '90s that the sexual revolution of the '60s is carrying enormously heavy consequences. The spread of sexually transmitted diseases grimly testifies to nature's bias against sexual promiscuity. The created order bears a moral coherence that is but a reflection of God's moral coherence.

2.43 "Assertion of the Raw Sovereignty of God in the Historical Process"

Without confidence that the world and its operations rest fundamentally on a moral order, there would be no point in crying out against injury and injustice. Why cry out in rage against unfairness and exploitation unless we are convinced that Someone hears us and that, while the millstone of God's justice may grind slowly, it grinds exceedingly fine? Prophetic religion asserts that God's power lies behind and in the unfolding of history. One of the messages of the prophets is that God will not forever tolerate the abuse of one's neighbors, especially if they are poor and lack social power sufficient to make their complaints heard. Brueggemann applies this prophetic theme to our own world when he says, "What if it is true? What if it is true that mocking God and abusing neighbor leads to the loss of land? Ask Mrs. [Imelda] Marcos, or ask the Somozas. One cannot generalize and say that it is everywhere, but you can easily make the case that we have before us practices of injustice that lead to land loss. Of course, people who have land always believe that it cannot happen here."[13] This is but one example of biblical religion's confidence that God works through history, redeeming it and directing it toward God's desired ends.

2.44 "Capacity for Discerning Social Analysis and Criticism"

In the eyes and hands of the prophets biblical religion goes beyond the voicing of complaints. It is surely important to cry out, to assault heaven with the shout that all is not well. But the prophets also move beyond complaint to analysis. They ask pointed questions. Why are things the way they are? What are the causes of our pain? What are the sources of injury and injustice? Nor are the prophets satisfied with the jargon and platitudes of privileged rulers and bureaucrats. Jeremiah refuses to be bought off by Hananiah's bland assurances that no harm will befall Jerusalem. The pat answers of the common theology are unsatisfactory. Thus Job stubbornly rejects the conventional theological wisdom of his three comforters. Biblical religion resists "conventional wisdom or theology" and insists on a deeper, penetrating wisdom for interpreting life and describing the response that the people are to give.

2.45 "Bold Conviction about an Alternative Possibility that Goes Under the Name of Hope"[14]

Hope is not hype. It is not the wish to be released from present trials and problems. Biblical hope dares to believe that God has alternative possibilities in mind. Biblical hope dares to believe in a future when "all things are made new." The hope-filled men and women of the Bible cry out to God that God's power will transform their present pain and difficulty into a new, redeemed situation. When in Egyptian bondage, Israel cried out to Yahweh in hope for a new day. In Babylonian exile Israel hoped for a deliverer.

From the cross, in his hour of anguish and radical loneliness, Jesus cried, "My God, my God, why hast thou forsaken me?" In this cry of dereliction there rings not a note of despair but of hope, for how can one ask of God to whom one prays why that God has "forsaken me" except in the hope that this prayer will be heard? The people of God cry out to God in the midst of their hurt, not in wailing despair but in hope that God will bring forth new possibilities—an exodus, a return from exile, a resurrection. The people who dare to cry with such hope are the people who make history.

2.5 God and Revelation

2.51 Revelation in the Bible

Theologians who attempt to write a complete, coherent, and systematic theology have made many claims about and arguments for the idea of revelation. In the context of biblical theology, which is the purpose of this text, we will do well to begin our reflections on the topic of God and revelation by asking the question, "How does revelation get treated in the Bible?"

The Greek and Hebrew words that the English Bible translates with the word "reveal" have as their root meaning "to uncover," as in to remove a veil. What is revealed was formerly unknown, inaccessible, or only partially understood. At the moment of revelation the veil or cover is lifted and we see. God, subject, actor, and narrator of the Bible, is beyond our ability to easily understand. Scripture often describes God in terms that are transcendent (see, for example, 1 Tim 1:17; Ps 19; Isa 6:1–8). The content of scripture is stories about the actions of this difficult-to-grasp God in relationship to persons. These actions are profoundly beyond our ability to readily grasp. We know God only as God chooses to be known, that is, as God reveals himself to us.

The problem we are describing is not restricted to knowledge about God. People often have difficulty in grasping ideas or problems because, at first, they are abstract. After further explanation, a story, or perhaps an illustration, we understand. At the moment of discovery or insight we often exclaim, "Oh, now I see!" In the Bible, knowledge is often closer to the meaning that results from insights than to knowledge that comes from the acquisition of propositions or information. When something is revealed, we see it. More than the product of accumulated rationality, biblical knowledge is perception; it is seeing the way things really are.

What sorts of things are "uncovered" in the Bible? On one level, any hidden, unknown or misperceived idea or thing can be revealed. Ideas and promises are uncovered. Thus we have 2 Samuel 7:18–29, a prayer addressed by King David to Yahweh. In the middle of this prayer David says, "For you, O Lord of hosts, the God of Israel, have made this revelation to your servant" (v 27). What follows is the covenant between Yahweh and David, wherein God promises David that his dynasty will be blessed and continue forever. Sin is another candidate for revelation. Job 20:27 reads, "The heavens will reveal their iniquity." Daniel 2 carries the famous story of Daniel's interpretation of the dreams of the Babylonian King Nebuchadnezzar. Several times in Daniel God is described as the one who reveals secrets. God gives humans wisdom that such secrets or mysteries might be disclosed.

Most important, however, is the understanding that biblical religion primarily deals with the disclosure or self-revelation of God. In 1 Samuel 3 we have the familiar story of Yahweh's calling of the boy Samuel. In this divine self-disclosure, Samuel sees what Yahweh is about to do: "Then the Lord said to Samuel, 'See, I am about to do something in Israel that will make both ears of anyone who hears of it tingle' " (v 11). Then Yahweh unveils for Samuel his intentions for Israel and especially the house of Eli. The chapter concludes with this striking summary, "The Lord continued to appear at Shiloh, for the Lord revealed himself to Samuel at Shiloh by the word of the Lord" (v 21).

Although humans cannot see Yahweh and live, God reveals himself to people through his words. Thus in 2 Samuel 3:21, the Lord was revealed to Samuel by God's word. God's words disclose or unveil God. This is the case because of the special relationship that the Hebrew mind understood to exist between speaker and speech. Far from being empty, words carried the vitality of their speaker or bearer. Indeed, "a word once uttered takes on a life of its own beyond the control of the speaker and achieves its effect by a kind of innate power."[15] This belief helps explain the ominous importance of blessings and curses in the Bible. It also explains why the Old Testament prohibits the use of the Lord's name in vain; to speak or otherwise use the name of the Lord in vain is to mis-appropriate the power resident in that name, gaining an ille-gitimate power through its use. The important point here is to see that the words themselves are not the revelation. Words are the medium of revelation. Yahweh is revealed through his word. Another way of stating this is to say that it is Yahweh who is revealed through Yahweh's words.

The works of Israel's great prophets offer the clearest expression of the relationship between Yahweh's words and revelation. The phrase "the word of the Lord" is commonly used in the Old Testament, and especially in the prophetic literature, to describe the manner in which God's will is revealed to Israel. It is certainly the case that several of the prophets refer to visions as the medium of revelation. Even in these cases, however, the word of the Lord typically accompanies the prophet's vision.

The Great Commandment begins with the *shema,* the Hebrew word for "listen" or "hear." "Hear O Israel: The LORD is our God, the LORD alone. You shall love the LORD your God with all your heart, and with all your soul, and with all your might" (Deut 6:4–5). "By his word spoken to the prophets, God makes known, not the elaborate information about the supernatural order ... but his righteous will, concerned with man's conduct in the world."[16]

Another point to be observed about God's revealed word is that it often casts what is to be revealed into the future. Yahweh reveals to Samuel what God is about to do in Israel. Isaiah 40:5 looks forward to a future day when "the glory of the Lord shall be revealed." The New Testament continues the idea of revelation as a future disclosure, as in Luke's reference to "the day that the Son of Man is revealed" (17:30) or Romans 8:19: "For the creation waits with eager longing for the revealing of the children of God." Although he does not use the word we translate as reveal, Paul's familiar words certainly carry this same idea of a future disclosure: "For now we see in a mirror, dimly, but then we will see face to face. Now I know only in part; then I will know fully, even as I have been fully known" (1 Cor 13:12).

2.52 Revelation and Our Life Setting

The story of God's dealings with the world remains incomplete and unfinished. It will remain incomplete as long as God continues to work among men and women within creation. It will remain incomplete until God rings down the final curtain on history. That God continues to be at work in the world seeking its redemption carries some important implications for our idea of revelation.

We tend to look at the Bible as if it *contains* the revelation. We often talk as if that revelation were a *thing* rather than *a way of seeing*. When we think of the Bible and revelation as a thing or object, we create a distance between our life setting and the world of the Bible. Then we believe that our task as readers of the Bible is to unlock the revelation *in the text.* Instead the study of the Bible shapes our character and vision so that the ongoing work of God in the world makes sense to us; the present-day activity of God is revealed and made meaningful to our lives.

The understanding of revelation as disclosure or unveiling is readily extended to include enabling the people of God to see what God is doing or is about to do. The Bible's intention is to form a people capable of answering faithfully the question, "What kind of people is God calling us to be?" To be a people capable of answering such a question, the church must possess the discernment to see what God is doing.

Such discernment rests largely on tradition and interpretation. Without the traditions of the past, without the Bible, it is scarcely possible to perceive what God is doing or about to do. This claim does not lock us into rote repetition of history and past traditions. Rather, it assumes that when God does a new thing, when unveiled, it will be consistent with God's past actions. Tradition and narrative are but other terms for the record of these past actions.

The Book of Isaiah contains many speeches or "prophetic oracles" in the form of poems celebrating the new thing God is about to do for Israel. The images of these poems frequently are drawn from a moment in Israel's past when Yahweh brought the people home from a previous long and bitter exile.

For example, Isaiah 41:17–18, part of a prophetic oracle addressed to Israelites captive in Babylonia, draws upon the Exodus for the imagery that the oracle employs to comfort and give hope to exiles hundreds of years after the Exodus and hundreds of miles removed from Egypt. In the midst of a desert wasteland, Yahweh promises to "make the wilderness a pool of water, and the dry land springs of water" just as he did through Moses during Israel's journey through the wilderness toward Canaan.

In chapter 43 Isaiah, in a striking parallel to the Exodus, describes the new thing God is about to do in the express terms of Israel's previous deliverance by his hand:

> Thus says the LORD,
>> who makes a way in the sea,
>> a path in the mighty waters,
> who brings out chariot and horse,
>> army and warrior;
> they lay down, they cannot rise,
>> they are extinguished, quenched
>>> like a wick;
> Do not remember the former things,

> or consider the things of old.
> I am about to do a new thing;
>> now it springs forth, do you not
>>> perceive it?
> I will make a way in the wilderness and
>> rivers in the desert.
>>>> (Isaiah 43:16–19)

Isaiah declares a word of the Lord that reveals that God is about to do something new in Israel. This new thing stands in continuity with an *old* thing: God's previous revealing actions and words. Those who remember what God had done in former days will possess the capacity to discern God's action in the present. They interpret the present in terms of God's redemptive action in Israel's past, actions that are told in the stories of God at work calling Israel out of bondage and into covenant fellowship with God. Israel's prophets possessed clear and detailed memories of Israel's past. It is not merely coincidental that the greatest of these prophets, Jeremiah, delivered prophetic sermons that closely resemble elements of the Book of Deuteronomy, the theme of which may easily be labeled "Remember."

Revelation in the Bible carries the idea of unveiling or disclosure. Often God's will or intention for the future is revealed. Israel's perception of this will requires a discernment that rests on the people's collective memory. This memory, in turn, is largely contained in the narratives and traditions that record Yahweh's mighty deeds. Even the Torah was written not by lawyers but by narrators, for there is no more fundamental way to talk of God than by means of story. Formed by this story, lives begin to conform to the God who is the central subject of this story. We have the reference points to see where God is at work in the places and times where we live. With such insight, we can align ourselves with this work, entering into it as the church, the body of Christ.

2.6 God and the People of God (Community)

2.61 God and Covenant in the Old Testament

Religion differs from magic.[17]

The distinction between magic and religion is important because of an apparent similarity between them. The apparent similarity leads persons to confuse one with the other leading to profound misunderstandings about the nature of God and the nature of God's relationship with humankind. One important difference is that magic claims to possess knowledge of the powers that govern the universe and the techniques to make them serve human interests. Magic claims to have power over these forces; the magician uses this power to force the powers to serve humans.

Religion, on the other hand, does not attempt to coerce divinity. Indeed, while in magic humans are the center of attention, in biblical religion, God is the center of attention. Both the religions of Judaism and Christianity focus their attention on God. While often attempting to get God to do their bidding, humans soon learn that God will not be coerced. Thereby they learn to interpret their lives in relation to God.

The first question of the Westminster Shorter Catechism puts this matter quite appropriately: "What is the chief end of man? The chief end of man is to serve God and enjoy him forever." This is not to say that the Bible thinks humans are unimportant. While God clearly is central to the meaning of human life and history, the Bible portrays God as unwilling to live alone. In the Bible we find God seeking a people with whom to live in a relationship of fidelity and love. Humanity is not the central character of biblical religion, but humans clearly are the object of God's search. "This is the mysterious paradox of Biblical faith: God is pursuing man. It is as if God were unwilling to be alone, and He had chosen man to serve Him. Our seeking him is not only man's but also His concern, and must not be considered an exclusively human affair. His will is involved in our yearnings. All of human history as described in the Bible may be summarized in one phrase: God is in search of man."[18]

One of the very first stories in the Bible portrays God searching for Adam and Eve in Eden. "When Adam and Eve hid from His presence, the Lord called: Where art thou? (Gen 3:9). It is a call that goes out again and again. It is a still small echo of a still small voice, not uttered in words, not conveyed in categories of the mind, but ineffable and mysterious, as ineffable and mysterious as the glory that fills the whole world."[19] God will not leave Adam and Eve alone in the Garden. The terrible disclosure of their sin begins in God's desire for fellowship with them in the Garden in the cool of the evening.

Repeatedly, throughout the pages of the Bible, God calls humans into fellowship. In Genesis 12 God states for the first time the great promise that in chapter 15 is articulated as the covenant between God and Abraham. God later covenants with Noah and with Moses. Joshua later asks the Israelites assembled at Shechem to choose whether they will put aside their idols and serve the Lord, according to the covenant between Yahweh and Abraham. In the New Testament Jesus reminds his disciples that they did not choose him; rather, he chose them. God first chooses and then relentlessly pursues

Israel through the pages of the Old Testament. Although they faithlessly play the harlot, Yahweh will not give them up to their own evil.

Thus Yahweh is nearly beside himself with grief when he cries in Hosea 11:8,

> How can I give you up, Ephraim?
> How can I hand you over, O Israel?

God will have this stubborn, stiff-necked people for his own, to love and cherish in life together.

The term that expresses the very essence of the relationship between God and the people of God is "covenant" (*berith* in OT Hebrew; *diatheke* in NT Greek). In the Bible, and especially the Old Testament, a covenant is "a solemn promise made binding by an oath, which may be either a verbal formula or a symbolic action. Such an action or formula is recognized as the formal act which binds the actor to fulfill his promise. Covenants may be between parties of different socio-political groups, in which case the covenant creates a relationship between them regulated by the terms of the covenant."[20]

In Genesis 15 Yahweh makes specific promises to Abram. Although he and his wife Sarai are childless, Yahweh promises that their descendants will be as numberless as the stars in the heavens. Yahweh promises even further that the land in which Abram has sojourned will one day belong to his descendants. These promises were solemnized through a symbolic act. At Yahweh's instruction, Abram slaughtered a heifer, a female goat, a ram, a turtledove, and a pigeon. He then split the carcasses of the heifer, goat, and ram, arranging them on the ground in two rows with a passageway between them and adding the carcass of one bird to each row. "When the sun had gone down and it was dark, a smoking fire pot and a flaming torch passed [down the row] between these pieces" (Gen 15:17). The act of passing between the rows of split carcasses sealed Yahweh's promises, as verse 18 continues, "On that day the LORD made a covenant with Abram...." By this covenant Yahweh binds himself to Abram and, through him, to Israel. But no less are Abram and Israel bound to Yahweh. Yahweh's "covenant lays claim to the whole man and calls him to surrender with no reservations."[21]

The covenant between Yahweh and Abram was greatly elaborated between Yahweh and Israel as it was restated between the Lord and Moses at Mount Sinai. The Ten Commandments are an example of the way in which Israel's fidelity to Yahweh is given greater specificity than had been the case in Yahweh's covenant with Abraham. An even greater elaboration of the terms of the covenant occurs in the so-called "covenant code" found in Exodus chapters 21—23. In fact, Exodus 19—23 summarizes the expansion of the original covenant. The setting of the narrative is the aftermath of the Exodus and the miraculous deliverance at the Red Sea. Yahweh instructs Moses to lead the people to Mount Sinai where Israel and the Lord pledge their covenant loyalty to each other. Unlike the covenant between Abraham and Yahweh, the covenant at Sinai includes the word *if:* "Now, therefore, if you obey my voice and keep my covenant, you shall be my treasured possession out of all the peoples. Indeed, the whole earth is mine, but you shall be for me a priestly kingdom and a holy nation" (19:5–6).

This covenant might have been—and occasionally was—Israel's strength. It unified the tribes that, after settling in Canaan, tended to go their own separate ways. Out of the covenant rose the Torah, the shared themes of Israel's history, and a common form of worship. When she lived in covenant-love and fidelity to Yahweh, Israel was theologically and ethically healthy and unified. But Israel could be—and often was—tempted into infidelity. The gods and the worship practices of the Canaanites tempted Israel away from Yahweh's covenant. The institution of monarchy tempted Israelites into a desire for a king "like the nations," thereby rejecting Yahweh and their peculiar form of covenant life with him. The prospect of possessing wealth and power tempted Israelites to treat their own people unjustly, fundamentally violating the terms of Yahweh's covenant.

The fact that Israel often violated Yahweh's covenant may lead us to conclude that this covenant was nothing more than a legal relationship based on a *quid pro quo* ("one thing in return for another") arrangement. In this view Yahweh promises to be Israel's God only because Israel offers obedience to Yahweh in return. One hears the dominant voice of this conditional side of the covenant especially as the relationship between Yahweh and Israel is elaborated in the covenant with Moses and again in the covenant Joshua restates at Shechem. *If* Israel is obedient and walks with the Lord according to the Torah, *then* will Yahweh walk with Israel in covenant fellowship.

We should not, however, allow this conditionality to obscure the equally valid and perhaps more important point that the covenant between Yahweh and Israel is purely a matter of grace. Referring to this covenant as it was formed between Yahweh and Abram, Walter Brueggemann says, "Here the covenant is simply a promise. It is one-sided as a commitment on the part of God to Abraham and exacts no comparable allegiance from Abraham to God. It is a commitment of free grace. The unqualified commitment of God in [Gen 15] verses 18–21 has its counterpart in verse 6. In both passages it is affirmed that God's movement toward Abraham is free and unconditional. Abraham need only trust."[22]

That Yahweh's covenant with Israel was simultaneously conditional on Israel's obedience and also purely a covenant of grace is surely one of the great paradoxes of the Old Testament and perhaps of all of biblical religion. We do not easily understand how both aspects can be true at the same time. On the one hand Yahweh appears to say to Israel, "We can live together; you can be my people and I will be your God, but only as long as you satisfy certain conditions and these are spelled out in the Torah." On the other hand Yahweh seems to promise Israel an unconditional love. No matter how often she wrongs him or spurns him for Canaanite idols, God will still redeem Israel—if only a remnant. How can both interpretations be true? "This incongruity is evident already in Exodus 34:6–7, which is a very old pivotal text in which God says in the mouth of Moses, 'The Lord, the Lord, a God merciful and gracious, slow to anger, and abounding in stead-fast love and faithfulness, keeping steadfast love for thousands, forgiving iniquity and transgression and sin.' All the great words are there: merciful, gracious, slow-to-anger, steadfast love, faithfulness, forgiveness, yet, 'who will by no means clear the guilty, visiting the iniquity … to the third and fourth generation.' Those two verses contain a massive contradiction that is at the heart of biblical faith."[23]

It may well be that people with a strong doctrine of holiness have a greater appreciation of the *if* side of Yahweh's covenant with Israel. Jesus' parable of the prodigal son illustrates the point. The story is too familiar to require retelling here. At its conclusion the prodigal's older brother, the one who has fulfilled his familial obligations and kept covenant with his father, registers his disapproval of the father's unconditional love of the wastrel. After all, the younger son not only squandered his inheritance but also broke the commandments. The younger brother disregarded the conditional if that his older brother took great pains to obey. Most of us, if we are honest with ourselves, make better sense of the older brother's obedience than we do of the father's unconditionality.

Fred Craddock tells a story about a time when he taught a Sunday school class and gave this parable a different ending. In Craddock's version, "the son came home and said, 'I am no longer worthy to be one of your sons. Make me one of your hired servants.' Then his father said 'That's right, you are not, so get on down to the barn and get to work!' At that point somebody in the back of the class said, 'That is the way it should have been told.' "[24] Of course, in Jesus' hands the story comes out in such a way that both sons enjoy the love of their father, regardless whether their relationship finally rests in conditional obedience or unconditional fidelity. In this beloved parable and in the narratives of Israel's often stormy relationship with Yahweh, paradoxically, both the conditional and unconditional aspects of Yahweh's covenant are present.

2.62 God and Covenant in the New Testament

Given the enormous significance of covenant as the defining term of relationship between Yahweh and his people in the Old Testament, it seems at first glance a little odd that the term occurs so infrequently in the New. But the word covenant raised problems for first-century Christians. Among Jews it had come to refer exclusively to the Mosaic law and the requirements of conditionality. Among Romans the Greek word used to translate the Hebrew *berith* meant an illegal secret society. Christians could not afford to use a word that carried two connotations that could so easily lead to wide-spread confusion. The word *diatheke* therefore occurs only thirty-three times in the New Testament and many of those are quotations of the Old. However, "on the basis of the little evidence available, one may conclude that, for a time at least, the early Christians did regard themselves as a community bound together by covenant, but that this covenant is a most free, creative reinterpretation of the older [OT] traditions."[25]

The central text of the New Testament that points to the Christian use of the term covenant occurs in Luke 22. Here we have the narration of the Last Supper:

> Then he took a loaf of bread, and when he had given thanks, he broke it and gave it to them, saying, "This is my body, which is given for you. Do this in remembrance of me." And he did the same with the cup after supper, saying, "This cup that is poured out for you is the new covenant in my blood."
>
> (Luke 22:19–20)

In other New Testament references to the Lord's Supper (Matt 26:28; Mark 14:24; and 1 Cor 11:25), "the blood is very specifically stated to be related to the [new] covenant, with obvious reference to the blood of the old covenant in Exodus 24:8. In light of the covenant forms, there seems to be no reason to doubt that this act was intended as the formal rite which established a covenant relationship."[26]

Jesus' blood shed on the cross becomes the basis of the new community, the church. Paul, writing to the Corinthians, says that Christ's death for all enables those who live in him to "live no longer for themselves, but for him who died and was raised for them" (2 Cor 5:15). Jesus' death and resurrection constitute the new community, the church, composed of those who are in Christ and by virtue of that relationship also live differently with and toward each other. The observance of the Lord's Supper becomes the central act of the new people of God called the church. For Paul, the Supper and Christian life in the new Christian community are inextricably linked.

As in the Old Testament, so also in the New, the idea of covenant entails the ethical obedience of the people of God. In his exegesis and interpretation of 1 Corinthians 11:17–34, Peter Lampe contends that Paul drew a clear connection between the church's celebration of the Lord's Supper and ethics.[27] Indeed, Lampe observes that Paul often discusses the ordinances when faced with the necessity of correcting misconduct. The Apostle often connects ordinances such as baptism and the Lord's Supper with the ethical life of the church. In the specific case of 1 Corinthians 11:17–34, Lampe establishes three possible Pauline connections between the church's ethics and the proclamation of the Lord's death in the ordinance of communion.

(1) Christ died for the weak; therefore, the strong Christians at Corinth should neither demean nor offend their weaker brothers and sisters.

(2) The Lord's Supper represents Christ's self-denial on the cross for the benefit of others. In view of Christ's example, the wealthy Corinthians should not ignore the hunger of the poor.

(3) The Lord's Supper establishes a close relationship between us and Christ's suffering.

In this ordinance we die with Christ. Paul also says that

baptism is a kind of dying with Christ. Those who in this manner participate in Christ's death by the same act commit themselves to lives of self-denial and love for others.[28] The celebration of the Lord's Supper is thus a "sanctifying ordinance," in William Willimon's terms. It is a symbol of God's grace active in the lives of the church. "Our characters are formed, sanctified, by such instruments of continued divine activity in our lives."[29]

In the Old Testament Israel was bound to Yahweh by covenant. The great paradox of Old Testament religion is that Yahweh's covenant with Israel was the product of God's sheer love and grace toward Israel and that the covenant was contingent on Israel's performance of its covenant obligations. Christians continued the use of the idea of covenant. Jesus refers to the cup of the Lord's Supper in connection with his own blood of the new covenant, the gracious gift of God's salvation. Like the Old Testament covenant, the new covenant in Christ's blood also has an ethical dimension. Those who walk with the Lord, those who are in Christ, God expects to live in a particular manner. Paul explains this point in 2 Corinthians. Whether in Old Testament or New, God searches for a people to walk with him in covenant relationship. Both gracious and conditional, the covenant is the basis for the community of God's people—no covenant: no community.

2.63 The Life Setting of the Covenanted People of God

People worship in churches and are affiliated with local congregations for many different motives. Some join congregations because it is socially acceptable. Others would never think of not attending church or being part of a local fellowship of believers; to them it is simply the right thing to do. People join churches looking for fellowship or that elusive sense of "community" that many social analysts say has disappeared from much of American life. Others attend church because they are seeking answers to some of life's personal, most persistent, and threatening questions.

These are the sort of questions that missiologist Paul Hiebert dubbed "middle range questions:" "questions of the uncertainty of the future, the crises of the present life, and the unknowns of the past.... How can I be delivered from illness? Why did my child, so full of enthusiasm for life, die so suddenly?"[30] Many people affiliate with churches in search of answers to these questions or to have other human needs met.

Commonly we come to church as individuals. We come as needy men and women seeking answers to our own questions and the fulfillment of our own needs. In America, under the persuasive influence of our society's individualism, people only rarely participate in church out of a sense of obligation to a gathered community of fellow believers. Doubtless there are folk for whom their sense of obligation to the larger body is a primary factor in their congregational participation. Such persons are a decided minority. American individualistic participation in congregational life obscures for us the Bible's long-term conception of the people of God as a community.

One of Paul's great metaphors for the church is the "body." This metaphor is more than a decorative figure of speech. He did not think of the church as a collection of individual men and women. Rather, he thought of men and women as extensions of the church, the body of Christ. Christians draw their individual vitality and their mission through their life in the church, where the Spirit orders life and gifts people for their own ministries.

The church, then, is a community that is *prior to* our individuality. As Christians we are grafted into Christ through salvation. Since we are in Christ we also are grafted into Christ's body, the church. To be saved is to be born into the body, the new community, the new people of God, the church. Yet we tend to think of the church—especially the local congregation—as the product of our individual wills, a kind of socially contracted body.

Another example of American individualism's influence on us is the way we read the Bible. The word *you* we typically interpret in the singular and therefore personally. The majority of the instances of this word in the Bible, however, whether in Hebrew or Greek, actually take the plural form. The term *you* in the Bible most commonly refers to the whole people of God, the community of the faithful.

If we take seriously the Bible's understanding of the people of God as God's covenanted community, some of our assumptions about the church and its setting in life may require expansion. We are not suggesting that our current understanding and practice of church-life is wrong or misguided, but rather, that they can be more complete. To be sure, the church is to be the source of comfort and consolation in time of grief and need. It is the purpose of the church to meet the human needs of people. One can summarize this point, in H. R. Niebuhr's fine phrase, by saying that the purpose of the church and its ministry is the increase of the love of God and neighbor. The challenge for the church, as for Israel of old, is to align ourselves with the purposes of God, who desires that all people should know and serve him. It is this last point where our understanding and practice of the church can be expanded to a more complete vision.

Yahweh's covenant with Israel and, by extension, the church is the fundamental basis for our walk with the Lord. The Bible seeks to teach us how to walk in that way. Christian discipleship is fundamentally a matter of learning to live in covenant relationship with God who is the central figure of scripture. We cannot advance far in that walk apart from life together in the body of Christ. As we follow in discipleship to the Lord, we come to see the church as far more than a place to have our needs met. As we grow in the faith we come to see the church, the new people of God, as the community through whose practices we learn to see our lives from the larger framework of God's redemptive purpose for individual lives and for the life of the world. We learn to see and interpret the meaning and purpose of our lives from the perspective of God.

Notes

1. Walter Brueggemann, "Genesis" in *Interpretation: A Bible Commentary for Teaching and Preaching* (Atlanta: John Knox Press, 1982), 25.

2. Walter Brueggemann, "First and Second Samuel" in *Interpretation: A Bible Commentary for Teaching and Preaching* (Atlanta: John Knox Press, 1990), 50.

3. John Bright, *A History of Israel* (Philadelphia: Westminster Press, 1959), 272.

4. Joseph Blenkinsopp, *A History of Prophecy in Israel* (Philadelphia: Westminster Press, 1983), 24.

5. *Ibid,* 25.

6. cf. Walter Brueggemann's four lectures on the Book of Jeremiah, delivered as the Newell Lectures sponsored by the Center for Pastoral Studies of the School of Theology, Anderson University, "Jeremiah: Faithfulness in the Midst of Fickleness." In Timothy Dwyer, Ed, *The Newell Lectureships,* vol II (Anderson, Ind: Warner Press, 1993), 13–72.

7. *Ibid,* 33–34, passim.

8. The term is used by Walter Brueggemann to represent theologies that order life in a narrow understanding of God's sovereignty that tends to serve the interests of the wealthy and powerful, and "which regularly identifies the order of creation with the current social arrangement so that the system is the solution." *Old Testament Theology: Essays on Structure, Theme, and Text* (Minneapolis: Fortress Press, 1992), 4–5, 22.

9. *Ibid,* 25.

10. Walter Brueggemann, *Hope within History* (Atlanta: John Knox Press, 1987), 55.

11. *Ibid,* 57.

12. *Ibid,* 80–81, passim.

13. *Ibid,* 1.

14. *Ibid,* 69.

15. sv "Word" in *Interpreters' Dictionary of the Bible,* vol 4 (Nashville: Abingdon, 1962), 3.

16. "Faithfulness in the Midst of Fickleness," 29.

17. "Magic" here refers to the mysterious art called conjuring. By magic we do not mean the illusions of modern entertainers, but rather the human effort to grasp the processes by which the world operates and bend them to the will of the magician. The Bible acknowledges the presence of such persons, for instance, the "Magi" of Matthew's nativity story and Simon Magus ("the magician") of Acts. Clearly, such persons worked in magic for reasons besides its entertainment value.

18. Abraham Heschel, *The Prophets* (New York: Harper and Row, 1962), 3.

19. *Ibid.*

20. sv "Covenant" in *Interpreters' Dictionary of the Bible,* vol 1 (Nashville: Abingdon Press, 1962) 714.

21. Walter Eichrodt, *Theology of the Old Testament,* trans by John Baker (London: SCM Press, 1962) 714.

22. Brueggemann, "Genesis," *150.*

23. Brueggemann, "Faithfulness in the Midst of Fickleness," 35.

24. Cited in Brueggeman, *Ibid,* 39.

25. "Covenant," 772.

26. *Ibid.*

27. Lampe, "The Eucharist: Identifying with Christ on the Cross," Interpretation 48/1 (January 1994), 36–49.

28. *Ibid,* 44–45.

29. Willimon, *The Service of God,* 125.

30. Quoted in Richard J. Mouw, *Consulting the Faithful* (Grand Rapids: Eerdmans), 1994.

Chapter Three

Israel

—Merle Strege—

When Abram was ninety-nine years old,
the Lord appeared to Abram, and said to
him, "I am God Almighty; walk before me,
and be blameless. And I will make my
covenant between me and you, and will
make you exceedingly numerous." Then
Abram fell on his face; and God said to
him, "As for me, this is my covenant with
you: You shall be the ancestor of a multitude of nations. No longer shall your name
be Abram [that is, exalted ancestor], but
your name shall be Abraham [that is,
ancestor of a multitude]; for I have made
you the ancestor of a multitude of nations.
I will make you exceedingly fruitful; and I
will make nations of you, and kings shall
come from you. I will establish my covenant
between me and you, and your offspring
after you throughout their generations, for
an everlasting covenant, to be God to you
and to your offspring after you. And I will

give to you, and to your offspring after
you, the land where you are now an alien,
all the land of Canaan, for a perpetual
holding; and I will be their God.

God said to Abraham, "As for you, you
shall keep my covenant, you and your offspring after you throughout their generations."

—Genesis 17:1–9 (NRSV)

3.0 The Christian and the Old Testament

If the Bible is the great story of God, Israel, Jesus and the
church, then a course of study on the Bible must consider the
people of Israel and their experience of God. To do so
requires careful study of the Old Testament, an assignment
that Christians are sometimes reluctant to pursue. They often
believe that the Old Testament is, just as its name suggests,
old, and therefore somewhat disconnected from the life and
experience of the *new* people of God, that is, the church.
Adult Sunday school class members will sometimes say that
they find the Old Testament irrelevant to their personal lives
and needs.

Thorough knowledge of the life and teachings of Jesus
begins in a careful study of the religious world that was his
home—the world of Judaism, nourished and sustained by the
narratives of the Old Testament. In fact the scripture used by
Jesus and the early Christian communities is what we call the
Old Testament. It is nearly impossible to understand Jesus
and the first-century church apart from the study of the Old
Testament. The disciples and earliest Christians perceived
their experience of the Risen Lord in light shed by the
Hebrew Bible. (After all, they did refer to him and think of
his lordship according to the Hebrew term "Messiah.") Out of

this inspired experience they wrote the New Testament.

Jesus uses the term "scriptures" in all four gospels. These scriptures are the Hebrew Bible, the Old Testament. The Apostle Paul frequently cited the Old Testament, quoting from the Septuagint. The early church's setting, when combined with Jesus' and Paul's use of the Old Testament scriptures, gives Christians ample reason to take them, and therefore Israel's experience as they record it, as the subject of serious study in their own right.

3.1 Israel and the Ancient World

To consider the place of Israel's experience of God and its role in biblical theology, we must begin by distinguishing history from theology. History is human experience in time and space; theology is the product of our reflection and interpretation of that experience with special reference to God. The Old Testament records Israel's interpretation of its experience of God at a lengthy but nonetheless particular moment—from the faintest recollections of humans down to the second century BC; and the Old Testament records Israel's interpretation of its experience of God at a particular place—the eastern end of the Mediterranean basin from the River Nile on the southwest to Asia Minor on the north, to the mouth of the Tigris-Euphrates Rivers on the east. In poetry, in law, in the sermons and oracles of the prophets, but especially in its narratives, the Old Testament gives us Israel's understanding of its experience and its special obligations as Yahweh's people. Before we can consider those reflections and the character of those obligations, we must first orient ourselves to the broader history and international politics of the world in which Israel lived.

In ancient times the eastern Mediterranean region was dominated by three great powers. First Egypt, then the Assyrian Empire, and finally the Babylonian Empire rose to economic and military prominence. Each of these great powers attempted to expand its sphere of political influence, especially in the western end of the area known as the Fertile Crescent (Palestine). This was one of the region's very few areas where agriculture could flourish. Land suitable for agriculture was extremely scarce and therefore an important political and military objective. So Egypt, Assyria and Babylon enlarged their territories at the expense of the much smaller and less powerful peoples who inhabited Palestine and the surrounding region. These were the Hittites, the Perizzites, the Amorites, the Canaanites, the Jebusites, the Hivites, the Philistines, the Syrians, and, after their entry into Canaan, the Israelites, as well as many others.

Much of the material of the Old Testament deals with Israel's experience from approximately 1200 BC to 400 BC, an eight-hundred-year period when the balance of power tipped back and forth among the three great empires. During the first part of this period all three lapsed into relative weakness, which created a kind of power vacuum in Palestine. This vacuum left a space in which the region's above-named "little people" contested each other for dominance. This was the era of Israel's greatness, the monarchy of Saul, David, and Solomon.

Greatness was followed by decline during the so-called divided monarchy, when the great prophets of Israel and Judah proclaimed their messages of justice and righteousness. About 800 BC a reinvigorated Assyria began expanding into Palestine, followed by a newly aggressive Babylonia. Assyrian aggression led to the destruction of the northern kingdom of Israel in 722–1 BC. After a period of especially cruel domination, the Assyrian Empire began to weaken and its armies were destroyed by the Babylonians and Medes at the Battle of Carchemish in 612 BC, one of the truly epochal battles of world history. After Carchemish no other nation possessed the military capacity to check Babylonian expansion. In 587 BC their armies marched into Jerusalem, burned the royal palace, a great deal of the city, and carried off into exile much of its able-bodied population.

Israel remained in exile until the Babylonians were overthrown by the Medes and the Persians in 539 BC under Cyrus. As the exiles began returning to Judah they rebuilt the temple between 520 and 515 BC. This is the era of some of the later prophets such as Haggai, Obadiah, and Malachi. Some time about 450 BC under the governor Nehemiah, the people of Judah rebuilt the walls of Jerusalem. This also is the era of Israel's great Torah scholar and advocate, Ezra. The Old Testament era closes and the intertestamental period begins during the years when the armies of the Greek conqueror Alexander the Great and his successors overran Palestine, dominating it until the Maccabean revolt of the 160s BC. This revolt brought freedom and peace to the region until the coming of the Romans approximately a century later.

Against the backdrop of international politics, amid the tumult of marching armies and war, in moments of economic prosperity and political greatness, in the depths of despair and hopelessness, in righteousness and corruption, Israel experienced the presence of God. This experience was not limited to the affairs of state and international power politics. Individual Israelites also experienced God in the affairs of everyday life: in their need for forgiveness for sin, in courtship and married life, in the world of work and leisure, in moments of high worship and personal inspiration, in relationships within extended families and among neighbors, in economic and property relationships, even in the matter of daily diet. Whether in public or private spheres of life, Israel experienced Yahweh's presence. The Bible's very existence rests in Israel's experience of God; apart from it there would be no Bible. Israel's poets, prophets, sages, and historians reflected on this experience, pondered its meaning for their lives as a nation and as individuals, and disputed their conclusions with each other. Out of this reflection a conversation extending over centuries produced the canonical books of the Old Testament. When we read and study these books, we are privileged to enter into Israel's experience with God. From this inspired community's experience the church still draws wisdom and inspiration for our life as followers of the Lord Jesus Christ.

3.2 Israel as the Community of God

Israel was a people before it was a nation. The people did not need national institutions, such as a monarchy, to give them an identity. They were a people because Yahweh chose them and covenanted with them to be their God. Israel's identity rested in the prior action and call of God. Yahweh had called *Israel* a people rather than a collection of individuals. Israel understood itself to be *the people* of God, not an aggregation of individuals who had made highly personal and individual decisions to follow Yahweh. Israel grasped her experience of Yahweh in a primarily corporate sense. This corporate dimension is sometimes difficult for modern people to understand or perhaps appreciate. An illustration from the Bible may clarify the point.

Joshua 7 tells the interesting and, to modern ears, troubling story of Achan, a man who sinned against the Lord, and this sin's consequence for his entire family. Achan's story begins in Yahweh's instructions governing Israelite conduct at the battle of Jericho. The Israelite warriors, Achan included, were expressly warned to "keep away from all things devoted to destruction, so as to not covet and take any of the devoted things and make the camp of Israel an object for destruction, bringing trouble upon it. But all silver and gold, and vessels of bronze and iron, are sacred to the LORD" (Josh 6:18–19). Achan disobeyed this command, took some of Jericho's forbidden plunder, and hid it under the floor of his tent. His sin went unnoticed among the Israelites until their next battle, when the Israelite army was routed and about thirty-six men were killed by a much inferior force from the city of Ai. Israel's army suffered defeat and men died because one man, Achan, disobeyed Yahweh's command.

After inquiring of the Lord, Joshua set about to learn the identity of the man who had brought calamity on the whole nation. Judgment followed swiftly upon Joshua's discovery that Achan was the guilty party. But not only Achan must atone for his sin: "Then Joshua and all Israel with him took Achan son of Zerah, with the silver, the mantle, and the bar of gold, with his sons and daughters, with his oxen, donkeys, and sheep, and his tent and all that he had" (Josh 7:24) to the Valley of Achor where they were stoned to death and their bodies burnt.

Among other lessons, this story makes the point that sin has consequences beyond the individual who sins. More remarkable, however, is the calm manner in which the story and everyone in it accepts the judgment that Achan's family must die along with him; not only his family, but even his livestock must suffer the penalty for Achan's sin. Few of us believe that we ought to serve the same prison sentence handed down to one of our relatives; we would think such a judgment to be an infringement upon our inalienable rights and monstrously unfair. No one of Achan's family utters even the first word of complaint. Everyone in the story accepts the verdict: one man sinned, everything connected with him is contaminated by his sin and must be destroyed. Nobody protests. Nobody raises a voice to say, "It's not fair! *I* didn't do anything wrong! *I* didn't disobey! Why are you stoning *me?*" How is it that the Israelites agree to a verdict that levels judgment against an entire family because of the sin of one person?

The answer to this question lies in Israel's understanding of the people as possessing what might be called a *corporate personality.* This phrase was coined many years ago by the Old Testament scholar H. Wheeler Robinson to capture a unique aspect of Israel's understanding of one person's relationship to the group.[1] Deuteronomy 26:5 is a text that Israelites learned to recite together when they brought their offering of the firstfruits to the temple for sacrifice.

That text reads in part, "A wandering Aramaean was my father." It refers to Israel's distant past, when they were a band of desert nomads. Robinson suggests that Israel's strong sense of the primacy of the group dates from those early days, for he says, "the desert is no home for the isolated individual."[2] Survival in the desert depends, now and even more then, on a strong sense of group solidarity. Robinson does not carry this notion to the extreme view that Israelite group consciousness swallowed up any appreciation for the individual person. Rather, Israelites thought of individuals as necessarily connected to the group, which consequently took priority over the individual.

In Israelite political theory, the nation did not exist by constitution or by act of a sovereign people who bind themselves together in a social contract such as the Plymouth colony pilgrims' famed "Mayflower Compact." Individual Israelites did not vote on the question whether or not to be a people or nation; as a matter of fact, they did not vote at all. Israel existed as a people through Yahweh's act of redemption in the Exodus and in the subsequent covenant made with the people at Sinai. "Yahweh was forever 'the out-of-Egypt-bringing-God' (as German theology might phrase it); Israel was the chosen people, linked to Him by no quasi-physical tie such as that of a nature-god, but by a moral act. It was this relation which … underlay the covenant of Yahweh with His people. The relation of moral obligation as well as of feeling has a special name (*hesed*) in Hebrew, which is inadequately translated as 'loving-kindness.' It means much the same as *agape* in the New Testament. Observe that the covenant is with the nation, not with the individual Israelites except as members or representatives of the nation. Throughout the whole period of the Old Testament, this covenant with the 'corporate personality' of Israel remains the all-inclusive fact and factor, whatever the increase in the consciousness of individuality."[3] Israel, in other words, thought of the group as prior to the individual. The dominant term Israel uses to express its idea of the community is "covenant."

3.21 Covenant and Community

We have already discussed the idea of God's gracious covenant with Israel. In chapter 1 we considered the covenant from the standpoint of God's gracious action; we looked at the covenant, so to speak, from God's side. We examined the three interpretations that Israelites gave to the idea of covenant. Some in Israel read the covenant as Yahweh's unconditional and eternal election of Israel as God's people bound in a covenant that could not be undone. Others, like the writers and prophets of the Deuteronomic tradition, interpreted the covenant as conditional upon Israel's obedience to Yahweh and especially Yahweh's Torah. A third view emphasized the unconditional graciousness of God who cannot let the people of God go. Here we want to consider another aspect of the covenant. This time, from Israel's side, we will pay particular attention to the Israelite sense of itself as the covenant community of God and the consequences for Israel of that covenant.

3.22 Fidelity, Obedience, and the Community

Deuteronomy 6:20–25 captures some of the essence of Israel's ideas about the education of its young. This education shaped people for life in the community of Israel. According to this text, the day would come when young Israelites would lose sight of the meaning that lay behind the elements of Israelite worship and ethics, which is but another way of saying life in the community of Israel. In that day Israelite children would ask their parents, "What is the meaning of the decrees and the statutes and the ordinances which the Lord our God has given you?" The text goes on to instruct the older generation in how to answer this question appropriately. Essentially, the parents—indeed all the members of the parents' generation as well as older generations—are instructed to answer their children's questions by reciting for them a highly condensed version of the story of the Exodus. But why tell a story in answer to the child's inquiry into the meaning of the symbols of Israelite worship and ethics?

For Israel, as we have already seen, there is no more fundamental way to speak of God than by means of story. Since Israel is the covenant people of God, the proper starting point for a discussion of Israel's religious and moral life will be in a recounting of the actions that Yahweh has undertaken in behalf of this people. The education of the young thus begins as the older generations recount the narratives of God that define and locate the Israelites as a community in relation to Yahweh and to the rest of the world. There is still more to be said about Israelite education, for the story of her walk with Yahweh served as the foundation of that education. Two important educational goals rested on this foundation in narrative.

Walter Brueggemann suggests that education among the people of the Old Testament occurred in two dimensions. In the first consideration, education in Israel is *education in passion.* "Education in passion … is nurture into a distinct community which knows itself to be at odds with [the dominant culture and its values and assumptions]."[4] Surrounding Israel were the various Canaanite peoples: the Canaanites, Amalekites, Perizzites, Jebusites, and others. These peoples formed a dominant culture that threatened to overwhelm Israel and its religion. The Old Testament repeatedly refers to the introduction of idols and the worship of Baal and Asherah, Canaanite fertility deities. From this we can infer a long struggle on the part of Israel to maintain itself as a separate people who were formed by their faithfulness to Yahweh. Israel knew almost instinctively that the education of the next generation was crucial to the community's ongoing survival.

In the case of Israel, education is more than the transmission of knowledge and information from one generation to the next. Rather, Israelite education operates on the assumption that the rising generation must be prepared for life *among* and *as* the people of God. This means that, indeed, there are certain matters that they must know, but even more they must come to understand themselves and interpret their lives in relation to the community. Israel is a storied people. They know who they are and what Yahweh expects of them on the basis of the narratives that tell the story of God. This story, and Yahweh's interaction with Israel recounted therein, shapes Israel and marks them as a different people. In the ritual admission to the congregation through the ceremony of *bar mitzvah* for boys and the *bat mitzvah* for girls, later Judaism has continued to practice the educational goal of accepting this difference. The phrase means "son or daughter of the commandment," and it is of course the commandments that form the core of the "decrees and the statutes and the ordinances" that Yahweh gave to Israel during its encampment at the base of Mount Sinai after the Exodus.

3.23 The Community of Moral Expectation

To be educated for membership in a community is to experience the slow and subtle shaping of one's character so that one will be capable of life according to the expectations of the community. In this sense, the people of God—whether Israel or the church—is a community of moral expectation. To live as part of Israel is to display a particular way of life that often put Israelites at odds with the cultures surrounding them. To be the covenant people of Yahweh marked Israel as different in its world. People who lived as part of the community of Israel were expected to possess characters that displayed certain virtues.[5] Those who are educated in passion come to acquire certain virtues that are characteristic of the people of God. Among these virtues are the following:

- *"The ability to cry, to feel pain, to articulate the anguish, to sense the pathos and act on it."*[6] It is one thing to hurt. It is quite another to be able to express that pain in terms that identify its source and therefore also indicate its remedy. Israel possesses this ability and, in its times of unfaithfulness, Israel also knows where to direct this cry. Israel falls into difficulty and even peril when it insists on managing its own affairs, trusting in its own abilities. The people are spiritually and theologically healthy when they remember that their cry must be directed to Yahweh.

- *"The ability to care, to welcome the stranger," as Deuteronomy 10:19 says, "Love the sojourner therefore; for you were sojourners in the land of Egypt."*[7] The golden rule taught by Jesus in the New Testament has its roots in Israel's sense of the neighbor's moral importance. Israel taught its children to care on the basis of this simple moral teaching: "You know what it feels like to be hurt, to be ignored, to be trampled down. Since you didn't like that experience, treat strangers and sojourners with the respect and hospitality you wanted when you were the victims and marginalized as a people."

- *"The ability to rage."*[8] At certain moments of its pilgrimage as the people of God, Israel dares to challenge what appears to them to be cases of Yahweh's indifference to them or to the covenant. So Israel's prophets and psalmists assault heaven itself with insistent demands of God, seeking an answer to the question of why the wicked prosper. These people insistently and impatiently inquire of Yahweh, "How long, O Lord?" Such insistence and impatience are virtues; too much submissiveness is a vice that leads to an excessive conformity to the status quo. Until the coming of the "new heaven and the new earth," the status quo should never satisfy the people of God.

• *"The ability to hope."*[9] Hope looks to the future and the new thing God seeks to do. Therefore, hope also serves to keep the present open and under review. The people of God are not permitted the attitude that says of the present that "it doesn't get any better than this." The tradition of hope causes "Torah-nurtured people" to be impatient, problematic, and difficult to administer.

Whether Israel or the church, these four abilities are virtues crucial to the character of the people of God. They are not the only virtues of the people of God, but they are surely among the most important. They certainly are evident as the desired characteristics of the community of Israel throughout the pages of the Old Testament. Through its recitation of the narratives of God's activity, Israel sought to form the characters of its young people so these abilities might come to be part of their own individual characters. Such abilities distinguished Israelites and enabled them to live faithfully as the community of Yahweh. By the same token, the absence of such abilities seriously compromised the Israelite community's faithfulness as the people of Yahweh.

We might consider the literature of the Old Testament prophets as a summary of Israel's goal of education in passion. The same might be said of much of the narrative portions of the Old Testament and many of the Psalms. Another

kind of literature can be found in the Old Testament, a literature that has an educational goal quite different from developing the abilities that gave the Israelite community its passionate character. This literature, the wisdom writings, offers an
education in perspective, the other great dimension of
Israelite community life. If education in passion formed Israel
with the character to cry, care, rage, and hope, education in
perspective, according to Brueggemann once again, "consists
in the older generation communicating its deposit of tested
perspectives to the younger generation, and one hopes, hav-
ing that younger generation appropriate that perspective with
respect and discipline." Israelite education in perspective also
aimed at developing four virtues of its own in the younger
generation:

• *"An appreciation of the coherent interrelation of life in
all its many aspects."*[10] In Israelite wisdom literature the
moral, spiritual, and physical worlds all fit together in one
unified whole. When Proverbs or the Psalms say that the fear
of the Lord is the beginning of wisdom, they do not mean to
suggest that only spiritual or religious knowledge is important. Rather, the fear of the Lord is the beginning of a comprehensive wisdom that includes the spiritual, the moral, and
the physical worlds. As the one creation of the one God, it
must be the case that these worlds are harmoniously interre-
lated.

• *"An acknowledgment of life's transcendent mystery
even in the midst of these relationships."*[11] Proverbs 30:4
asks a series of questions that criticize the claims to knowledge made by the wise sages. "Who has ascended heaven and
come down? / Who has gathered the wind in the hollow of his

hand? / Who has wrapped up the waters in a garment? / Who has established all the ends of the earth?" Since none can step forward to answer such questions, then wisdom obviously has its limits. The questions unmask the wise person's claims to know.

• *"Arrival at a trustful submission and yielding to Yahweh and Yahweh's ways."*[12] After working its way through the first three capacities of this list, the wisdom literature comes full circle. It asserts that there is a way of wisdom for the people of God. It will follow this instruction: "Trust in the Lord with all your heart, / and do not rely on your own insight. / In all your ways acknowledge him, / and he will makes straight your path. / Do not be wise in your own eyes; / fear the Lord, and turn away from evil. / It will be a healing for your flesh and a refreshment for your body" (Prov 3:5–8).

The people of Israel were the covenant people of God. That covenant relationship stamped Israel with a character unlike that of any of its neighbors. To be an Israelite was to be an extension of this community and thus to be educated in passion and perspective. The Israelites, then, were educated toward the goal of coming to live out those characteristics or virtues that, if realized, would enable them to live in faithful relationship to Yahweh. Thus Israel was a community of moral expectation, founded on the narratives recounting Yahweh's gracious actions on its behalf and formed through its understanding that their religious and moral life arose from those narratives. Through Yahweh's action and covenant on her behalf, Israel was to be a community unlike the other peoples of the earth, a peculiar people through whom all the nations ultimately would receive Yahweh's blessing.

3.3 The Covenant Community as the Just and Righteous Kingdom of God

Yahweh's covenant with Israel called the nation to be a community of justice and righteousness. However, "the very nature of her covenant faith had given Israel a deep sense of destiny as the people of God and, with it, the hope and the confidence that God would bless her and establish his rule over her in the Promised Land."[13] Distorted, this confidence became the royal or Jerusalem theology discussed in chapter 1. "The rise of the Davidic monarchy, although it drastically altered the tribal structure of Israel and made changes which effected every aspect of her society—changes bitterly resented by some—nevertheless made much of that hope a reality."[14] However, the monarchy's achievements and therefore Israel's political-military expansion, growing economic prosperity, and the development of stable social institutions, provided occasions for temptation even as they were causes for celebration. That Yahweh had made of Israel a great nation seemed beyond dispute, and now the question became, "Would all the hope of Israel, and all her sense of destiny, be transferred bodily to the Davidic state and find its fulfillment in terms of it? In short, would the Kingdom of God be made equal to the Kingdom of Israel?"

Israelite kings never were free in any final sense to set their own standards of law and morality. In Israel, Torah defined right and wrong for kings even as it did for the lowliest peasant. Indeed, Israelite kings were not even free to write their own job descriptions; Torah prescribed royal duties and prohibited royal excesses (compare Deut 17:14–20). Above all, "when he [the Israelite king] has taken the throne of his kingdom, he shall have a copy of this law written for him in the presence of the levitical priests. It shall remain with him and he shall read in it all the days of his life, so that he may learn to fear the LORD his God, diligently observing all the words of this law and these statutes, neither exalting himself above other members of the community nor turning aside from the commandment" (Deut 17:18–19). It is altogether clear that Israelite kings, including David who served as the standard for all the kings who followed after him, failed to live up to Torah's expectations. The kingdom of David and its successors fell short of the standard of the kingdom of God.

Israelite kings were often tempted to lower or even deflect people's expectations of the monarchy. But this was never a real possibility in Israel because of the presence of the great prophets. More than any other factor in Israelite religion or society, the prophets stood as representatives of Torah and the requirements it imposed on commoner *and* king. Since Torah disclosed the will of Yahweh, the prophets who spoke for Yahweh also defended Torah and reaffirmed its teaching. This role often cast the prophets as adversaries of the monarchy. David has his Nathan, Ahab his Elijah, Hezekiah his Isaiah, and Zedekiah his Jeremiah. The prophets stood on guard in Israel and Judah, ready to speak the word of Yahweh to kings and any others who dared to flout Yahweh's will. The prophets indict Israelites—king and commoner—for their failure to keep Torah and thus their infidelity to Yahweh's covenant. This failure and faithlessness clearly separate the kingdom of Israel from the kingdom of God.

3.31 Yahweh's Norms of Justice: The Jubilee Legislation

The principles of justice inherent in the covenant are broad and demanding, inclusive of the whole created order—not only the people but also the land upon which the people live.

Isaiah 61:2 (and therefore Jesus' quotation of this text in Luke 4:18–19) refers to "the year of the Lord's favor" or in the familiar words of the King James Version, "the acceptable year of the Lord." John Howard Yoder takes this phrase to be a reference to the jubilee legislation detailed in Leviticus 25. About this text Yoder says, "The place of Leviticus 25 in the Bible kept alive the vision of an age when economic life would start over from scratch; and the testimony of Isaiah 61 demonstrates its fruitfulness as a vision of the coming renewal.... That the renewal of God's people, both the concrete renewal which is possible and has happened occasionally in past history, and the renewal after the end of the age, will have the form of the jubilee is thus integral to the prophetical vision."[15]

The jubilee laws of Leviticus 25 must be understood as an attempt to prevent economic exploitation and promote justice. Torah raised barriers to this kind of exploitation because of its firm belief that the land itself belonged to Yahweh. Israel's economy was based on agriculture, and therefore the matter of land ownership was crucial. The jubilee laws saw to it that land reform became—or was intended to become[16]—a regular feature of Israelite economic life. As Yahweh says in Leviticus 25:23–24, "the land is mine; with me you are but aliens and tenants. Throughout the land that you hold, you shall provide for the redemption of the land."

Rest, for humans, for beasts, and for the land, is an underlying principle of the blueprint for Israelite economic life we find in Leviticus 25. After six years of sowing and reaping, Israelite fields and vineyards were to lie fallow for an entire year; "it shall be a year of complete rest for the land" (Lev 25:5). The fiftieth year, the Sabbath of sabbath-years, was to be dedicated to the Lord as the jubilee.[17] In that year, families were to return to their ancestral land holdings, the property allocated when Joshua had originally apportioned the land after the people entered Canaan (compare Josh 14—20). In the fiftieth year, all leases were to expire after a just and equitable financial settlement. The fiftieth year was also to bring the release of all those Israelites whom economic misfortune had forced to sell themselves into bond-service. Under no circumstances were Israelites to buy and sell their fellow Israelites as slaves; that would be to return to the dreaded oppression of Egypt. But in the year of the jubilee, "the year of the Lord's favor," even bond-servants were to be freed: "they shall go back to their own family and return to their ancestral property" (Lev 25:41). Every fiftieth year Israelite economic life was to rest from the pursuit of wealth, rest from a kind of acquisitiveness that forced some people into servitude, and rest the land from agricultural use. Thus the idea of rest was built into the very foundation of Israel's social and economic life.

The principle of rest and the assertion that the land itself belonged to the Lord are keys to understanding Yahweh's desire for the corporate and social shape of life in the reign (kingdom) of God. Israel had to be reminded, and often, that Yahweh owned the land and the people had been commanded to rest. Israel's life as the covenant people of God hinged on the commandments. Those commandments aimed at justice, righteousness, rest, and preeminently the reminder that Yahweh is Lord and none other. The commandments are voiced first in Torah; they are echoed in the prophets and in the wisdom writings, but the theme remains constant.

The address of God to Israel, echoed through so many human voices, asserts the ways of conduct that make life possible, that make available communion with God and peace with neighbor. God's address to Israel, variously mediated, is not heavy-handed coercion, but a gift that makes wholeness possible. The command of God and its mediation are indeed a gift of God's grace; we are made privy to the foundational requirements whereby God's good will is offered to us.[18]

Within the context of the jubilee year and by examining the themes of the prophetic oracles and their indictment of Israel's failures, we can begin to draw a picture of what the prophets believed were the chief characteristics of life in the kingdom of God. By identifying those characteristics then we can generally describe life in the community called the people of God.

3.32 Amos and the "Day of the Lord"

Amos, a shepherd from the Judean village of Tekoa, prophesied in the northern kingdom of Judah during the 8th century BC, probably about the years 760–750. He delivered his messages during the reign of King Jeroboam II, a time of unparalleled Israelite economic prosperity and territorial expansion. Both king and people could easily interpret these favorable conditions as signs of Yahweh's favor. But Amos rose to deliver a stern warning and, ultimately, judgment against Israel. One very interesting feature of Amos's preaching was the unique twist that he gave to a popular religious idea of the day, the "Day of the Lord."

Israelites of this era looked forward eagerly to the "Day of the Lord." They believed that this "day" would inaugurate an

age of peace and freedom from the aggression of their enemies. Israelites thus anticipated the Day of the Lord as a time
of lightheartedness, security, and celebration. They were
already prosperous; the arrival of the Day of the Lord would
add military security to their already abundant material life.
Amos stood this popular notion on its head. Thus he said,

> Alas for you who desire the day of the LORD!
>> Why do you want the day of the LORD?
> It is darkness, not light; as if someone fled
>> from a lion,
>> and was met by a bear;
> Or went into the house
>> and rested a hand against the wall,
>> and was bitten by a snake.
> Is not the day of the LORD darkness, not light,
>> and gloom with no brightness in it?
>> (Amos 5:18–20)

Far from unprecedented peace and prosperity, Amos interpreted the Day of the Lord as a time of unpredictable terror
and uncertainty. Why did Amos interpret this popular religious idea in such a radically different fashion?

Amos answers our question in 5:24: "Let justice roll down
like waters, and righteousness like an everflowing stream."
Yahweh's controversy with Israel, and thus the reason for
Amos's revised interpretation of the meaning of the Day of
the Lord, rests in the Israelites' failure to practice justice.
According to Amos's preaching, God is interested in justice
far more than in worship and praise (5:23–24). Evidently
prosperity had not reached to all classes in Israelite society,
and Amos condemned the rich for extravagant lifestyles purchased at the expense of poor farmers and shepherds. The
wealthy reclined on luxurious beds carved from ivory, loung-

ing idly through day and dining sumptuously without rising even to fill their drinking cups (6:4–6; 4:1). Such people "turn justice to wormword, and bring righteousness to the ground" (5:7) as they "trample on the poor and take from them levies [taxes] of grain" (5:11).

Fundamentally, then, Amos reinterpreted the Day of the Lord as a time of judgment for the nation's sins of injustice:

> For I know how many are your transgressions,
>> and how great are your sins—
> you who afflict the righteous, who take a bribe,
>> and push aside the needy in the gate.
> Therefore the prudent will keep silent in such a time;
>> for it is an evil time.
>
> (Amos 5:12–13)

According to Amos, Yahweh determined to punish Israel because it failed to observe the commandments that underwrote justice. The poor in Israel were treated unjustly by the rich, who exploited them to pursue lifestyles of ease and extravagance. We may conclude from this that Yahweh expected Israel to order its social and economic life in a way that would not benefit some at the expense of others. Life in the community of the people of God was to be characterized by fairness and benefit for all. Nor would Yahweh be satisfied with a trickle of justice or a dribble of righteousness; Yahweh willed that they flow through Israelite society with the irresistible force of a flash flood.

3.33 Isaiah and the Age of the Messiah

Isaiah lived in Jerusalem and preached there from about 740 to 700 BC. This time period includes the fall of Samaria, the capital of the northern kingdom of Israel, and its annexa-

99

tion by the reinvigorated Assyrian empire. The Assyrians were arrogant, brutal overlords. Amos describes them as leading away their captives by fish hooks (4:2). The Assyrians' conquest of Israel brought this feared people to Judah's doorstep. The Israelite buffer between Assyria and Judah had been wiped from the map and the residents of Jerusalem were alarmed and fearful of their futures. Like Amos, Isaiah attacked social injustice as the problem that strained the relationship between the people and Yahweh. He exhorted his listeners to place their trust in Yahweh rather than entangle themselves in international political alliances. Isaiah made such exhortations because of his unbounded confidence in Yahweh as the lord of history. Isaiah discerned God's hand in the unfolding of historical events, directing history toward its divine destiny. Thus Isaiah prophesied the coming of Messiah and the characteristics of the messianic kingdom.

> A shoot shall come out from the stump of Jesse,
>> and a branch shall grow out of his roots.
> The spirit of the LORD shall rest upon him,
>> the spirit of wisdom and understanding,
>> the spirit of counsel and might,
>> the spirit of knowledge and the
>> fear of the LORD.
> His delight shall be in the fear of the LORD.
>> He shall not judge by what his eyes see,
>> or decide by what his ears hear;
>> but with righteousness he shall judge the poor,
> and decide with equity for the meek of the earth;
> he shall strike the earth with the rod of his mouth,
> and with the breath of his lips he shall kill the wicked.
> Righteousness shall be the belt around his waist,
>> and faithfulness the belt around his loins.
>>>> (Isaiah 11:1–5)

Isaiah's prophecy gives us a picture of the messianic king. It also portrays the qualities that will characterize the reign of this king. The messiah's reign will bring righteousness and fairness for "the meek of the earth," for those impoverished people who have neither voice nor advocate. In other words, Isaiah described the messianic kingdom in terms similar to those marking the prophecy of Amos in the north. Beyond this similarity, however, Isaiah also described the messianic reign as a time when the spirit of the Lord would inspire the king with wisdom, understanding, counsel, and might. Unlike the reigns of the kings of Israel and Judah, laden with bureaucracy and fawning court officials, the messianic reign was *charismatic;* the spirit inspired and thus ordered life in the reign of the messiah. Near the very conclusion of the prophecy of Isaiah we find a summary of the characteristics of the messianic age, a description that Jesus repeated in the synagogue at Nazareth to inaugurate his public ministry. There the text reads:

> The Spirit of the Lord is upon me,
>   because he has anointed me
>   to bring good news to the poor.
> He has sent me to proclaim release
>   to the captives
>   and recovery of sight to the blind,
>   to let the oppressed go free,
> to proclaim the year of the Lord's favor.
>   (Luke 4:18–19)

Isaiah prophesied to a people who had broken their covenant with Yahweh. Their sins, both personal and social, had raised barriers between them and God. The people's hands were stained with blood. Their society degenerated into a corruption where the law courts were full of mischief and deceit. The people no longer lived in peace and justice. The hungry lacked bread, the homeless had no shelter, and the oppressed lost all hope of freedom (compare Isa 59:1–8; 58:6–7). The kingdom of David had become a sad parody of the kingdom of God. But the spirit of the Lord was to rest on one who would establish the kingdom of God and give a new birth of freedom, peace, justice, and righteousness—kingdom values one and all.

3.34 Micah and the Problem of Injustice

The blunt and simple farmer Micah lived during the same era as Isaiah although Micah was born some years later. So he knew something of the same political conditions that affected Judah and interpreted them in the same manner as Isaiah. But the two men were separated by an important fact of their existence. The great prophets of Israel came from all walks of life. Isaiah was a resident of Jerusalem and quite possibly a member of the upper class; Micah lived in the countryside at the village of Moresheth. The common element in their prophecy was the "word of the Lord," a word that came to each of them. Their prophetic responsibility was to declare this word to the people even when such declarations carried unpopular news. Micah prophesied against the religious and political leadership of Jerusalem and delivered to that city the terrible news that it would be destroyed by foreign invaders.

Yahweh's word to Micah announced judgment against Jerusalem. As with Amos and Isaiah, Micah understood the root causes of this judgment to lay in political and religious corruption. The wealthy and powerful laid in bed hatching schemes whereby they could use the law to seize farms and houses (Mic 2:1–2). Official court "prophets" used their office to deliver false messages of hope and comfort (3:5–7). Micah looked to the day when the peoples of many lands would eagerly seek Yahweh's torah and justice. That would be the day of Yahweh's *shalom* when the weapons of war would be reforged into farm implements. In that day farmers and small landowners would no longer worry that their land might be seized by the wealthy:

> But they shall all sit under their own vines
> and under their own fig trees,
> and no one shall make them afraid;
> for the mouth of the LORD of hosts has spoken.
> (Micah 4:4)

Until that day, however, Jerusalem and Judah could expect tribulation and, ultimately, destruction. The people failed in their obligations to one another, obligations that Yahweh laid down in a covenant that he was determined to enforce. This covenant defined Israel's relationship to Yahweh and the ethical and political norms of the Israelites' relationships to each other. To be sure, Israel lapsed into idolatry, and for such unfaithfulness, the lapsed people deserved punishment. But even a surface reading of the great eighth-century prophets discloses an equally strong judgment against the people for their failure to live justly and honorably toward one another. This failure also constituted a breach of the covenant, the charter document and blueprint of the kingdom of God and the community of the people of God as Yahweh originally intended. Micah aptly and succinctly summarized this side of the covenant when he asked, "What doth the Lord require of thee but to do justice, and to love kindness, and to walk humbly with your God?" (6:8).

3.35 Hosea, Jeremiah, and Israelite Faithlessness

In the Old Testament there can be no justice apart from righteousness nor righteousness without justice. Yahweh declares that he is uninterested in the worship of people who have acted unjustly toward their neighbors. With equal force Yahweh insists that an ethically upright life begins in *hearing* (and therefore *doing*) the commandments, which begin with the exhortation, "Hear! O, Israel: the LORD is our God, the LORD alone. You shall love the LORD your God with all your heart, and with all your soul, and with all your might" (Deut 6:4). Failure to follow this commandment rendered Israelite justice hollow. Life as the covenant community of God must begin in faithfulness to the Lord.

Two prophets saw with unusual clarity the importance of Israel's fidelity to Yahweh and the role of this fidelity in the establishment of justice in the land. Those prophets were Hosea and Jeremiah. They understood Israel's infidelity toward Yahweh with an insight and a poignancy unmatched in the pages of the Old Testament. They declared, respectively, to both northern and southern kingdoms, a message that disclosed the deepest of hurts in the very heart of God. The source of this hurt lay in the people's faithlessness to their covenant with Yahweh.

Hosea lived in the northern kingdom of Israel and prophesied during a slightly later period than Amos. These few years made all the difference in Israel's situation. While Amos prophesied during years of Israelite prosperity, Hosea made his appearance after the Assyrian army had begun its assault on both land and people. Society disintegrated before Hosea's very eyes. No fewer than four Israelite kings were assassinated within a fourteen-year period following the reign of Jeroboam II. In the face of enormous social upheaval and pain, Hosea stood forth to declare Yahweh's message of constant and redeeming love even to a people who had proved as unfaithful and inconstant as a prostitute. While we may find this metaphor offensive, it is precisely the one offered by Hosea himself. He took his own marriage to Gomer, "a wife of whoredom" (Hos 1:2), as a metaphor for Israel's disastrous, failed covenantal marriage with Yahweh.

As a result of this strange union, Gomer gave birth to three children. Although the text suggests that Hosea was not their father, at the Lord's command Hosea exercised the father's right to name them. The two younger children were given symbolic names of frightful, ominous import for the northern kingdom. One child, a daughter, was named *Lo-ruhamah,* ("Not pitied") "for I will no longer have pity on the house of Israel or forgive them" (Hos 1:6). The youngest of the three children Hosea named *Lo-ammi,* ("Not my people") "for you are not my people and I am not your God" (Hos 1:9). By their very names Gomer's children reminded the Israelites that they had fallen into the most desperate of situations. The ominous threat of Assyrian destruction could not be escaped if Israel were not pitied by Yahweh and, even worse, no longer the people of God.

Yahweh's controversy with Israel lay in her worship of the Canaanite fertility gods and goddesses. Although the circumstances by which this worship was introduced into Israelite life are less than completely clear, the Bible does report that some of King Solomon's non-Israelite wives returned to the worship of their ancestral gods in Solomon's old age (1 Kings 11:1–4); even the wise Solomon was not as true to Yahweh as his father David had been. After Solomon's reign ended and the kingdom divided, Israel's religious life deteriorated rapidly.

Most notorious in these long years of decline were King Ahab and his queen, Jezebel. During Ahab's reign both foreign queen and Israelite king worshiped the Canaanite god Baal: "Ahab did more to provoke the anger of the LORD, the God of Israel, than had all the kings of Israel who were before him" (1 Kings 16:33).

The worship of Baal and Asherah, his consort, included sexual intercourse with temple prostitutes, establishing a link between worshiper and the gods who were believed to control fertility—a crucial matter among agricultural peoples. Such actions flouted aspects of Israelite sexual morality, of course. Although it may seem odd to modern Christian consciences, to Israelites loyal to Yahweh the violation of the first commandment was a greater sin than the sexual impurity. Israelites who engaged in the sexual acts of Baal worship placed "other gods" before Yahweh in direct violation of the covenant. Hosea announced that Yahweh's judgment would fall heavily on such infidelity. Through the mouth of the prophet Yahweh says:

> She [Israel] did not know that it was I who gave her
>> the grain, the wine, and the oil,
> and who lavished upon her silver and gold
>> that they used for Baal.
> Therefore I will take back my grain in its time,
>> and my wine in its season;
> and I will take away my wool and my flax,
>> which were to cover her nakedness.
> Now I will uncover her shame
>> in the sight of her lovers,
> and no one shall rescue her out of my hand.
>> (Hosea 2:8–10)

Even in the face of Israel's shameless infidelity Yahweh's

great love finds a way to keep covenant with her. In one of the most moving passages of the Bible, God reminds the people:

> When Israel was a child, I loved him,
>> and out of Egypt I called my son.
> The more I called them, the more they went from me;
>> they kept sacrificing to the Baals,
>>> and offering incense to idols.
> Yet it was I who taught Ephraim[19] to walk,
>> I took them up in my arms;
>>> but they did not know that I healed them.
>>>> (Hosea 11:1–3)

> My people are bent on turning away from me.
>> To the Most High they call,
>>> but he does not raise them up at all.
> How can I give you up, Ephraim?
>> How can I hand you over, O Israel?
> How can I make you like Admah?
>> How can I treat you like Zeboiim? [20]
> My heart recoils within me;
>> my compassion grows warm and tender.
> I will not execute my fierce anger;
>> I will not again destroy Ephraim;
> for I am God and no mortal, the Holy One
>> in your midst,
>> and I will not come in wrath.
>>>> (Hosea 11:7–9)

Israel would undergo terrible chastisement for her unfaithfulness, but Yahweh's punishment contained within it the seeds of redemption.

More than a century after Hosea prophesied judgment and redemption in Israel, the prophet Jeremiah declared a similar message to the southern kingdom of Judah. Jeremiah delivered his messages against Judah and Jerusalem during the decades when Nebuchadnezzar and the Babylonian army threatened the theretofore unthinkable—the destruction of Jerusalem. Like Hosea, Jeremiah criticized the people for their worship of Canaanite idols, for the worship of any gods other than the Lord God of Israel. Jeremiah insisted that the covenant community must return to the faithful worship of Yahweh. Like Israel, Judah would have to face the judgment of the Lord. But beyond the coming destruction and exile was the promise of a new and more enduring restoration of the covenant.

The core of Jeremiah's theology and his complaint against Judah can be found in Jeremiah 30:1–40. This material is sometimes called the "Book of Consolation," dictated by Jeremiah to his secretary Baruch. These prophecies were delivered shortly before the destruction of Jerusalem in 587 BC. Their theme is destruction, yet Yahweh also promises healing and restoration. Life in Judah will not be as it was in the good old days before exile; it will be better.

> The days are surely coming, says the Lord, when I will make a new covenant with the house of Israel and with the house of Judah. It will not be like the covenant that I made with their ancestors when I took them by the hand to bring them out of the land of Egypt—a covenant that they broke, though I was their husband, says the Lord. But this is the covenant that I will make with the house of Israel after those days, says the Lord: I will put my law within them, and I will write it on their hearts; and I will be their God and they shall be my people. No longer shall they teach one another, or say to each other, 'Know the Lord,' for they shall all know me, from the least of them to the greatest, says the Lord; for I will forgive their iniquity, and remember their sin no more.
>
> (Jeremiah 31:31–34)

3.4 Covenant Community and Discipleship

What can Christians learn from Israel's experience? This may be but another way of asking about the relevance of the Old Testament for Christian teaching. Both Israel and the church illustrate the reality of chosenness. Israel is the *old* people of God; the church is the *new* people of God. Yahweh chose them both and chose them for intimate fellowship. The basis of this fellowship is covenant. The Old Testament Torah is the core of Yahweh's covenant with Israel; in the New Testament, Jesus' life, death, and resurrection form Yahweh's new covenant with the church. Christians affirm that the new covenant in Jesus fulfills the old. Basic to both covenants, however, is the idea of discipleship.

A disciple is a person who accepts the discipline of another. It is obvious that the two words come from a common root; disciple, of necessity, involves discipline. This discipline is not self-imposed. Master-teachers direct their disciples. Christians are most familiar with the idea of discipleship as it is portrayed throughout the gospels. Jesus invites his followers to accept the yoke of his teaching: "Take my yoke upon you, and learn from me; for I am gentle and humble in heart, and you will find rest for your souls. For my yoke is easy, and my burden is light" (Matt 11:29–30). But we may extend the principle of discipleship to the Old Testament as well. We may think of Israel as the covenant community of disciples and Yahweh as the teacher.

We commonly translate the word Torah as "law." While such a translation is accurate, it does not capture the full range of the meaning of Torah. More comprehensively, Torah means instruction. Thus Torah is more than a legal system of rules and regulations. Torah is instruction in walking in the way of Yahweh. If Israel would be Yahweh's people, they must walk in Yahweh's way. If Israel is to walk in the way of the Lord then it must be instructed in that way.

Exodus 19 tells the story of the beginnings of Israel's discipleship to Yahweh. The people are camped at Rephidim, still celebrating their miraculous deliverance first in the Exodus and second in Yahweh's miraculous defeat of the Egyptian army at the Red Sea. After centuries of oppression Israel was suddenly free, free of slavery and oppression, free of the fear of being captured and taken back to Egypt in chains. Israel was radically free, free as the sirocco, the desert wind that blows wherever it will. At this glorious moment, Yahweh directs Moses to march the people to the base of Mount Sinai. Israel's instruction is about to begin.

At Sinai Israel learns that Yahweh has not brought liberation for their sake or enjoyment. For the people of God, freedom is not an end in itself. The people of God enjoy freedom, but this freedom has purpose. Thus Yahweh orders Moses to tell the Israelites, "You have seen what I did to the Egyptians, and how I bore you on eagles' wings and brought you to myself. Now therefore, if you obey my voice and keep my covenant, you shall be my treasured possession out of all the peoples. Indeed, the whole earth is mine, but you shall be for me a priestly kingdom and a holy nation" (Exod 19:4–6). Israel responds to this divine declaration: "Everything that the Lord has spoken we will do" (19:8). The covenant between Yahweh and Israel is reaffirmed and Yahweh descends to Mount Sinai, where he delivers the Ten Commandments to Moses. Yahweh has begun to instruct Israel in the altogether important matter of living as the people of God.

This instruction continues for nearly one full year, the period of time that Israel remains encamped at Sinai. Here they receive Yahweh's instruction in how to live as the free people of Yahweh, the people with a divine mission to be intermediaries between Yahweh and all the peoples of the world. Only after the instructions have been given and the second Passover is celebrated will Israel break camp and begin its journey toward the Promised Land. When it departs, it leaves as the disciplined people of God who have agreed to live under the teaching of Yahweh.

Israel, of course, proves to be an unruly student under Yahweh's instruction. Even before the people crossed the wilderness they already had thrown off the Lord's yoke. They suffered the consequences of their refusal to walk in the way of Yahweh, but Yahweh's patience outlasted their perversity. Yahweh would still have this people and was prepared to chastise and wait until Israel accepted the yoke of Torah. The people's unruliness did not cease once they entered the Promised Land. The moral and religious ups and downs of the Israelites' forty-year journey through the wilderness were to be repeated in the nation's life after their establishment in Canaan—all the way down to exile and return.

Israelite discipleship lives between the two poles of its covenantal relationship with the Lord. On the one hand Yahweh insists that the people live according to Torah or suffer the consequences of disobedience. On the other hand Yahweh's absolute fidelity to Israel seems to bear any sin, any infidelity; if only the people will return they will find forgiveness. Israel's life of discipleship to Yahweh is paradoxically both conditional and absolute, as the great text of Exodus 34:6–7 says:

> The LORD, the LORD,
>   a God merciful and gracious, slow to anger,
>   and abounding in steadfast love and faithfulness,

> keeping steadfast love for the thousandth generation,
> > forgiving iniquity and transgression and sin,
> > yet by no means clearing the guilty,
> > but visiting the iniquity of the parents
> > upon the children and the children's children,
> > to the third and the fourth generation.

The Lord God declares these words to Moses on Sinai. They are alone together; the Ten Commandments are about to be delivered to Israel through Moses, the prophet unlike any other in Israel. Passing before Moses Yahweh makes the proclamation of Exodus 34:6–7. Then, the text says, "And Moses quickly bowed his head toward the earth, and worshiped" (Exod 34:8). To walk in the way of the Lord is wisdom, and wisdom begins in the "fear of the LORD" (Prov 1:7).

3.5 The Kingdom of God and the Kingdoms of this World

John Bright observes the tragic consequences that befell Israel when the people confused the kingdom of God with King David's political nation-state: "In other words, would Israel mistake the Davidic state for God's, and imagine that in it God *had* established his Kingdom?" After posing this question, Bright raises the possibility that the people of God in any nation may mistakenly confuse the goals of God's kingdom with the political aims of the state.

> That was Israel's question. It is a question which is neither ancient nor irrelevant, but is asked of us [in the United States] today. We are, it is true, in no external particular to be compared with the people Israel. But we, like them, are a people not very far from our origins, from the patterns of the past and the great faith of the

past—yet very far indeed. Like Israel we were lured on by a vision and a promise: a land of plenty, of freedom and human dignity. And we pressed toward that goal as if to that Promised Land "flowing with milk and honey." We have created a nation greater than David's, prosperity such as Solomon never dreamed of, and with it a complete metamorphosis of the national character. A few years have brought many changes.

So it is that the question before us is not unlike that which the monarchy posed for Israel. Perhaps, so far, it is only a question. But it is a question which cannot be evaded, and it matters greatly how we answer it. Will our destiny as a nation which calls itself Christian be satisfied in terms of the economic prosperity and the national might which we have created? Will we seek no higher salvation than the present order can provide in terms of increased income, automobiles and television sets? What is worse, will we, because we have churches and because our political forms are hospitable to their growth, assume that the present order is the God-ordained order which God—if he be just—may be called upon to defend always? The people that answer the question so, will see it as the sole function of religion to hallow in the name of God its own material best interests. But it will never begin to understand the meaning of the Kingdom of God.[21]

The Old Testament narrative of Israel's history serves to illumine the life of the church, the people of God, especially if the matter under discussion is discipleship. Unlike the church, however, Israel was more than a religious community. The covenanted people of Yahweh were also a nation-state. Nothing like the American separation of church and

113

state existed in ancient Israel. Whenever we begin to consider Israel as a forerunner of the church, we must remember this very significant fact. Israelite government and religion were part of one whole social fabric; they were not divided into separate spheres of influence.

We should not leap to the false conclusion that the contemporary people of God, the church, is immune to Israel's temptation to equate God's kingdom with its own political state. The great aim of the reign of God remains intact—*shalom.* This word encompasses and summarizes the primary virtues of the kingdom: faithfulness to God; justice, righteousness, mercy and compassion toward the weak; and a morality based on the commandments and the Sermon on the Mount. The people of God who forsake these great hallmarks of biblical discipleship for political and material prosperity have fallen into the same mistaken confusion as Israel of old. The people of God are ever beckoned toward the vision of life in communion with God according to the Lord's own instruction wherein we may walk in fellowship with Yahweh.

3.6 Covenanted Disciples: An Odd Community in the World

The covenant between Yahweh and Israel distinguished Israel from the other peoples of her world. On their best interpretation of the covenant, Israel understood itself to be a kingdom of priests, intercessors between their sociopolitical world and Yahweh. On their worst interpretation, Israel believed itself privileged and separate from other nations, God's chosen people. Correlative to both views is Israel's understanding that she was different. She was not to follow the religious beliefs and practices of her neighbors. The magnitude of differences between Israel and the other nations ranged from the major to the minor. Other nations practiced human, even child, sacrifice—an abomination in Israel. Israelites also observed a different set of dietary regulations and laws of ritual purification; foods considered normal by most of Israel's neighbors were forbidden to her people. In life's large and small matters Israel differed from her neighbors.

Part of Israel's difference lay in the utter dissimilarity between the God she worshiped and the gods of the surrounding nations. In distinction from her neighbors, who worshiped idols, Israel worshiped Yahweh, who was unseen and of whom absolutely no images were to be fashioned. The gods worshiped by Israel's neighbors were for the most part nature deities. They were believed to govern the natural cycles of birth, death, fertility and necessary components of nature like rainfall and sunshine. Israelites believed that Yahweh was Lord over nature, but they also believed that their God governed history. In this Yahweh was quite unlike the gods of Israel's neighbors. Yahweh's hand shaped historical events. Thus even the very name of the Lord, *Yahweh,* means, "I cause to be what I cause to be," Yahweh is the agent underlying the historical process *and* its meaning. In these respects, Yahweh was a god very different from the gods worshiped in the ancient near east. The people who worshiped Yahweh, of necessity, would also differ from their neighbors religiously and ethically.

Israel did not pursue a different course simply to be unique. Israel did not seek difference for its own sake. Indeed, at some points in its history, Israel sought policies and institutions that made it quite like the other nations: "Appoint for us, then, a king to govern us, *like other nations,*" the elders of Israel say to Samuel (1 Sam 8:5, emphasis added). Then, just as much as now, it is difficult to follow a life-course that marks us as odd. Most of us want to fit in, to be normal. Nevertheless, to walk with Yahweh according to Torah inevitably yielded the consequence that Israel would clearly differ from her neighbors in both religious and ethical practices. As Yahweh differed from the gods of her neighbors, so the people of Israel would be a different, somewhat odd, people. One might say that an important consequence of Israel's covenant with Yahweh was a religious and ethical role counter to the prevailing culture. Israel was not called to. be counter culture, *per se*. She was called to be the people of Yahweh, and that calling committed her to a counterculture life among the peoples of the ancient world.

Israel's life in its setting, its life of discipleship in the instruction of the Lord, if faithfully practiced would mark Israel as odd among its neighbors. Holiness, justice, righteousness, identification with the weak, the powerless, and the outcast, and, above all, her practice of ethical monotheism separated Israel from her neighbors. The life of discipleship to Yahweh inevitably distinguishes the Lord's followers from those who do not follow. Jesus, a true son of Israel, taught a very similar point; one cannot love God and mammon, that is, the world. This divine insistence that Israel is to be different raises important questions for the church, the new people of God. One then wants to ask, "What are the marks that distinguish the church from our nonbelieving society and neighbors? Does discipleship to Jesus and the God revealed in him still yield as an unavoidable consequence a community that is different? If so, what are the signs of this difference?"

Notes

Two books by Old Testament scholar John Bright take up the historical and the theological aspects of Israel. Bright's study of a prominent theological motif in both the Old and New Testaments is titled *The Kingdom of God* (Nashville: Abingdon, 1953); and he also wrote a magisterial account of Israel's history titled *A History of Israel* (Philadelphia: Westminster, 1964, 1980).

1. *Corporate Personality in Ancient Israel* (revised edition), Introduction by Gerber M. Tucker (Philadelphia: Fortress, 1980).

2. *Ibid,* 47.

3. *Ibid,* 51.

4. Walter Brueggemann "Passion and Perspective: Two Dimensions of Education in the Bible," *Theology Today* (July 1985), 173.

5. The terms character and virtue are used here with a specific meaning that differs from the way they are used in everyday speech. By character we mean a person's self, the quality about a person that is predictable, as for instance when we say, "You can count on Mary" or "You just can't count on Mike." Either positively or negatively, the sentences reveal to their listeners something important about these persons. Everyone, good or bad, thus has a character, a self-in-relation wherein such qualities as can be predicted reside. In our time virtue has come to be a virtual synonym for good. If someone says, "John is a virtuous man," we typically understand that sentence to mean "John is a good man." Interestingly enough, the term virtue has come to have a narrower range of meaning when applied to women. Thus the sentence "Mary is a woman of virtue" often is understood to mean that Mary's sexual morality is above question. Classically, however, the term virtue means the quality that enables a person or object to fulfill its purpose or function. The purpose of a knife is to cut and a knife's virtue thus would be the keenness of its blade. Applied to humans, the term means those excellent qualities that enable humans to live their lives as human life was originally intended. For a fuller account of these terms and their relationship to morality and Christian education, see the essays "Walking with God: the Church and Morality" and "History as a Moral and Political Art" in Merle D. Strege, *Tell Me the Tale: Historical Reflections on the Church of God* (Anderson Ind: Warner Press, 1991), and also "The Bible, the Church and Christian Education' in Merle D. Strege, *Tell Me Another Tale: Further Reflections on the Church of God* (Anderson, Ind: Warner Press, 1993).

6. Brueggemann, quoted in Strege, *Tell Me Another Tale,* 167–68.

7. *Ibid.*

8. *Ibid.*

9. *Ibid.*

10. *Ibid.*

11. *Ibid.*

12. *Ibid.*

13. *Ibid.*

14. *Ibid.*

15. John Howard Yoder. *The Politics of Jesus*, 2nd edition (Grand Rapids: Eerdmanns,1994) 28–33.

16. *Ibid,* 31.

17. There is no indication that Israelites ever practiced the jubilee laws as regular elements of their economy. The fact that they went unobserved does not, however, lessen their force any more than disobedience to the commandment prohibiting adultery makes it impractical.

18. Brueggemann, *Finally Comes the Poet: Daring Speech for Proclamation,* (Minneapolis: Fortress, 1989), 80.

19. Another name for Israel.

20. Admah and Zeboiim were cities of the plain destroyed along with Sodom and Gomorrah.

21. Bright, *Kingdom of God,* 43–44.

Chapter Four

Jesus

—Richard Willowby—

He is the image of the invisible God, the firstborn of all creation; for in him all things in heaven and on earth were created, things visible and invisible, whether thrones or dominions or rulers or powers— all things have been created through him and for him. He himself is before all things, and in him all things hold together. He is the head of the body, the church; he is the beginning, the firstborn from the dead, so that he might come to have first place in everything. For in him all the fullness of God was pleased to dwell, and through him God was pleased to reconcile to himself all things, whether on earth or in heaven, by making peace through the blood of his cross.

—Colossians 1:15–20, (NRSV)

4.0 Which Jesus?

Popular theology, and indeed theological sentiment throughout much of Christian history, leads to the statement, "We know what God is like because we know what Jesus is like." Martin Luther once remarked that we should look at the face of Jesus and affirm, "This man is God." This idea finds perhaps its highest expression in Colossians' ringing statement that Jesus is the "image of God." The Greek word used here for image is *eikon* (the English word icon), expressing the strongest possible connection between Jesus and God.

The books of the New Testament present us with related but different images of Jesus. The language of Colossians speaks of the relationship between Jesus and God in terms of identity. John's gospel opens with its prologue statement, "And the Word was God" and later recounts Jesus' own saying that "I and the Father are one" (10:30). Yet the New Testament also makes other, very different, statements about Jesus. The Acts of the Apostles records Peter's sermon on Pentecost, where he says to the Jerusalem crowd.

> You that are Israelites, listen to what I have to say: Jesus of Nazareth, a man attested to you by God with deeds of power, wonders and signs that God did through him, as you yourselves know—this man, handed over to you according to the definite plan and foreknowledge of God, you crucified and killed by the hands of those outside the law. But God raised him up, having freed him from death.
>
> (Acts 2:22–24)

The New Testament presents us with several images of Jesus that, taken together, make a multifaceted portrait.

Since New Testament images of Jesus vary, we should not be surprised to find varied images of him throughout the long history of Christianity. Historian Jaroslav Pelikan has written an elegant book in which he identifies nearly twenty different images of Jesus that captivated people's attention at one moment or another in the history of western culture. Jesus has been "rabbi," the "universal seed of reason," "the crucified one," "the Prince of Peace," "the Bridegroom of the Soul," and many others. Clearly, Christians across the centuries have been captivated by one or another aspect of the Jesus we find in the pages of the New Testament.

In the face of these multiple perspectives, how do we come to any certainty about Jesus?

Three different sources of authority combine to answer the Christian's search for certainty. First of all we have the gospel portraits of Jesus. The Bible is the canonical witness to God's self-disclosure in historical events, and, as the Letter to the Hebrews opens,

> Long ago God spoke to our ancestors in many and various ways by the prophets, but in these last days he has spoken to us by a Son, whom he appointed heir of all things, through whom he also created the worlds
>
> (1:1–2)

Second, Jesus promised the presence of another to take his place in the world. Christians affirm that the Holy Spirit is the continuing, inspiring presence of God in Christ that teaches us directly. Third, the church as the body of Christ and bearer of the Great Commission carries the responsibility to teach the Scripture in the empowering presence of the Spirit. We answer the question, "Who is Jesus?" through the combination of these three sources of Christian life and thought.

The witness of all three sources is interwoven and must be interpreted together. We have the Jesus of the Gospels. We have the Holy Spirit. We have the teaching and practices of the church. Jesus is of no great consequence if he is limited to the thirty years he walked the dusty roads of Palestine and not alive in us through the Holy Spirit. By the same token, then, as it deals with a person's walk with the resurrected Christ, the leading of the Spirit must be sifted and corroborated by what we know of Jesus through both the biblical witness and through the church's teaching and practice.

We cannot know Jesus by ourselves; we know him only through the joint witness of church, Bible, and Spirit. Therefore we may initially answer the question, "Which Jesus?" with the statement: The Jesus we speak of is the resurrected Christ made known to us through the Bible's witness, the illuminating power of the Holy Spirit, and the teaching and practice of the community of faith, that is, the church, the body of Christ.

While we may first hear the name of Jesus from parent, friend, or teacher, nevertheless, all discussion of him begins with the biblical narrative of his life and teachings. There is no more fundamental way to speak of God than by means of narrative. When we speak of God by means of narrative, then, all that we say about God is measured first against what we learn in Scripture. The same is true for what we say of Jesus. Scripture forms the foundation of our discussion and our search; scripture stands as the measuring stick against which all dialogue about the person of God, the authority of Jesus, and the role of the Holy Spirit is measured.

An often told and perhaps apocryphal story tells of an American reporter's conversation with the great Swiss theologian Karl Barth. This interview took place late in Barth's life.

One of the major twentieth-century influences on Christian theology and religion, he was asked to state the most important idea he had learned in all of his years of study, teaching and writing. His answer: "Jesus loves me, this I know for the Bible tells me so."

The great stories of Jesus' life wait for us in the biblical text. They are our stories and the stories of the church. Across the centuries the stories of Jesus have formed the church and certainly determined the meaning of the word "Christian." From the Bible we learn Jesus' agenda—his mission.

> The scroll of the prophet Isaiah was handed to him.
> Unrolling it, he found the place where it was written:
>> "The Spirit of the Lord is on me,
>> because he has anointed me
>> to preach good news to the poor.
> He has sent me to proclaim freedom for the prisoners
>> and recovery of sight for the blind,
> to release the oppressed,
>> to proclaim the year of the Lord's favor."
>
> Then he rolled up the scroll, gave it back to the attendant and sat down. The eyes of everyone in the synagogue were fastened on him, and he said to them, "Today this scripture is fulfilled in your hearing."
>> (Luke 4:17–21)

Stories like this tell us how Jesus related to his followers and what he thought important. We learn how he understood the application of the Law and how he responded to authority. We learn the ethical teachings of the Sermon on the Mount and some of the ways Jesus himself applied them. We learn what he thought about the purpose of life, the power of prayer, the authority of believers, and the appropriate treatment of friend and foe. In his teachings, his relationships, and his parables, Jesus set forth the foundations and design within which the community of faith continues to understand itself.

To approach the beginnings of an adequate answer to our question—"Which Jesus?"—there are certain understandings that must be clear, especially if that answer is to reflect the biblical record. These understandings have to do with what we know about Jesus and the nature of the written record.

4.01 What We Know of Jesus

Jesus' life spanned three decades of the first century in a rural culture in a remote province of the Roman Empire. He was born in Bethlehem of Judea during the last years of Herod the Great, the child of Mary and Joseph of Nazareth. He was born a Jew and was raised according to the Law of Moses. As an infant, Jesus was circumcised and presented in the temple at Jerusalem. Because of threats on his life, he and his parents moved to Egypt and safety. He returned to Galilee after the death of Herod and lived in Nazareth. At the age of twelve, he was taken to the temple as tradition required. Other than the stories that surround his birth, we know nothing more about the early years of Jesus. The gospel accounts of his life are quite uninterested in the years of his adolescence and young manhood. They do not pick up the thread of his life story until approximately his thirtieth year.

Jesus did not travel far. Most of his active teaching years were spent in the relatively confined area of Galilee. The villagers and common folk of that region called him "Rabbi," for he taught clear and sometimes radical ideas about the nature and the reign of God. He taught with authority and attracted a large following within which could be found a smaller group of his disciples. He enjoyed real popularity among the common people as seen in the large crowds his appearances produced. His teachings about the kingdom of God called all people, young and old, rich and poor, upper-class and commoner, to a life of single-minded devotion to Yahweh, whom he referred to, in the Aramaic of his day, as "Abba," best translated with the familiar "Daddy." He worked miracles of healing and exorcism that freed people from the bondage of illness, possession and death. He claimed to be the Son of God and was an arch critic of a certain kind of Pharisaism that practiced a form of legalism that he believed contradictory to the heart of Torah. His teachings were accessible to common humanity because he taught in stories called parables. These teachings that often seemed to treat the Law too casually brought him friends *and* enemies. He was frequently challenged and threatened but never trapped or caught—until the end.

Jesus was probably thirty-three when he went to Jerusalem for what would be the last time. Through intrigue, lies, and betrayal, he was arrested, tried, and sentenced to death as a result of his own words taken out of context, twisted, and turned against him in a secret trial. He died a criminal's death by crucifixion. If the story ended here, we would most likely not be talking or writing about him today.

The story, of course, does not end here. His followers and the church understood the life, birth, and death of Jesus in radically charged ways. For they perceived that Jesus of Nazareth was also Yahweh's Messiah, a term meaning the "Anointed One" that was translated into the equivalent Greek term, *Christos*, the Christ. Over time this apostolic witness led to the further understanding that Jesus was both fully God and fully human. Without reference to the sophisticated theology of later centuries and under threat of persecution, earlier generations of Christians learned to refer to their participation in his resurrected life by the sign of a fish, a sign that commonly identifies Christians to this day. The Greek word for fish is *ichthus*. Christians used it as an acronym, its letters forming the first letters of their affirmation of who Jesus was and what he had done on their behalf: "Jesus Christ, God's Son, Savior."

The stories and traditions we have from the gospel period began as stories orally passed along from believer to believer until an urgency developed for a written account. Those who knew Jesus personally were suffering martyrdom for their new faith. Their personal knowledge of the Lord became crucial to the preservation and spread of his teachings. Even with this urgency, however, not everything that happened, not all that was said, and not all that was done was recorded. Twice in John's Gospel the incompleteness of the narratives is stated. First, in 20:30 John says, "Now Jesus did many other signs in the presence of his disciples, which are not written in this book." Later, at the very end of his gospel, John tells his readers,

> Jesus did many other things as well. If everyone of them were written down, I suppose that even the whole world would not have room for the books that would be written.
>
> (21:25)

We do not know all that might have been known about the earthly life of Jesus of Nazareth. We do not know all that the earliest Christian community knew and thought about Jesus of Nazareth. What we do know of him and his life is sufficient for salvation.

4.02 The Nature of the Written Accounts

Although some people think of the gospels as biographies, in actuality they are far from it. A biography is a carefully researched and highly detailed account of the life of a person. The purpose of biography is historical; biography intends to open up to our understanding the thought and action of its subject. The goal of contemporary biography is the presentation of the most balanced and unbiased view possible of the subject. The gospels, however, are not balanced in that sense; they are written from a very clear and intentional bias.

The intentional, purposeful nature of the Gospels makes it appropriate to think of each of them as a sermon. That they might be much longer than you would wish to hear on a Sunday morning makes no difference; they are sermons nonetheless. In fact, the writers of the gospels are often called evangelists, a term that comes from the English transliteration of the Greek word *euangelos*. The term simply means the "good news" or gospel, and evangelists therefore are messengers who spread this good news. Whether from a pulpit or a computer keyboard, the evangelist is the one who announces or otherwise carries the good news and paves the way for people to hear and know it.

In light of the word *euangelion,* the gospels of the New Testament are not impartial biographies but highly individual portraits of Jesus that aim to teach and preach, that is, proclaim, the good news of Jesus. While the gospels do contain historical and biographical information as well as the teachings of Jesus, their aim is not to secure or otherwise reflect on Jesus' place in history, but to secure a place for Jesus in the lives of people. These evangelists write to give a defense and to convince. As the evangelist John says, "[what is written in this book is] written that you may believe that Jesus is the Christ, the Son of God, and that believing you may have life in his name" (20:31). The evangelists who wrote the canonical gospels aimed not at authentic history, but at authentic, changed lives.

The Gospels and the church affirm that Jesus is the center of our existence. Writing about the Gospel of John, Ernst Kasemann said,

> John is concerned with one theme only, which he continually varies: to know him is life. That, then, is the one question that he asks his readers: Do we know Jesus? Everything else fades into twilight and darkness; it loses its importance and is pushed aside. [People] and the world become important only so far as they have to do with him, just as God is made known to us only through him.[1]

The New Testament writers and the people in their narratives focused on Jesus. Their stories and the evangelists' thoughtful, prayerful, and inspired reflection provide the primary basis for what we know about the Jesus who walked and talked on the roads of Galilee. Their accounts witness that this same Jesus rose from the grave, ascended into heaven, and communes with his followers through the promised Holy Spirit. He is the same Jesus who called a few humble men to leave their fishing nets and follow him; the same Jesus who wept when Lazarus, his friend, died; the same Jesus who, looking at a Roman coin said, "Give to Caesar what is Caesar's and to God what is God's."

If we would know Jesus we must come to know him in and through the stories he told and the stories told by the gospel witness about him. If we would know Jesus we must know him through his church, which the inspired Apostle Paul called the very body of Christ. If we would know Jesus we must know him through his Holy Spirit. If our lives are to be transformed by an experiential knowledge of Christ, we must open our lives to him in every way available to us.

4.1 Jesus and Redemption

Scripture tells us that the followers of Jesus saw him as redeemer. The church historically declares Jesus to be the redeemer. In faith all believers declare "Jesus is my redeemer." Often words and phrases like saved, converted, or "have accepted Jesus" are used to describe that which is accomplished in and for us through the redemption made possible by Jesus.

Various theological accounts explain in different ways the essential aspect of redemption, but each theory affirms certain common and fundamental understandings about the nature of Jesus the Redeemer.

- Jesus died for the salvation of humanity (John 3:14–18).
- Jesus died as a substitute for humanity (Matt 20:28).
- Jesus died to turn the wrath of God away from humanity, thereby reconciling humanity with God (2 Cor 5:18).
- Jesus died to redeem humanity (1 Cor 6:19–20).
- Jesus died to "declare God's righteousness" (Rom 3:24–26).

Deeply imbedded in Jewish culture and religious life is a metaphor that aptly catches up each of these dimensions and connects the Old and New Testaments at the same time. We find the metaphorical phrase in this declaration from John's Gospel: "Behold, the Lamb of God, who takes away the sin of the world" (John 1:29). This powerful reference perceives

Jesus and his life in terms of the rich heritage of the religious traditions and especially the sacrificial system of the Hebrew people. John Bright helps us to see the significance of this connection.

> As the covenant at Sinai united the twelve tribes to one another about the service of the common God, so did [the Lord's Supper]. In it Christ identified his followers with himself: the people of the Lord God of Israel have become in the New Covenant the people of the Servant. Here, too, the number twelve is significant; how important it was is clear from the speed with which another was elected to take Judas' place (Acts 1:15–26), for the symbolism of new Israel must be preserved. And if a covenant must be sealed by a sacrifice, here the sacrifice is the Servant himself: 'This cup is the New Covenant in my blood.' It was only right and natural that the church should identify Jesus with the Passover sacrifice (e.g. 1 Cor 5:7) and hail him as 'the Lamb of God, who takes away the sin of the world' (John 1:29; compare Heb 12:24; 1 Pet 1:19; 2:24; compare also Isa 53:7, 10). In this sacrifice has the whole sacrificial system of the Old Covenant been fulfilled and superseded.[2]

We can find the theological and religious account of the sacrificial system detailed in Leviticus. There Torah specifies its requirements for the forgiveness of sin. The fundamental assumption lying behind these legal prescriptions is that "without the shedding of blood there is no forgiveness of sins" (Heb 9:22). This statement is found in the Letter to the Hebrews, where we find an extended treatment of Jesus' redeeming death in light of the Hebrew sacrificial system. That system required the blood sacrifice of an animal in order that sin might be forgiven. A sacrificial victim's blood needed to be shed because, in the language of Leviticus 17:11, "For the life of a creature is in the blood, and I have given it to you to make atonement for yourselves on the altar; it is the blood that makes atonement for one's life."

Leviticus 4 details the sacrifices that purchase the forgiveness of sin. An anointed priest who sins brings guilt on the whole people of Israel and therefore must present an unblemished bull as a sin offering to Yahweh (4:3). The entire assembly of Israel might sin unintentionally, perhaps a sin of omission, and thereby incur guilt on all the people. They may be forgiven if they make an acceptable sacrifice: "The elders of the congregation shall lay their hands on the head of the bull before the Lord, and the bull shall be slaughtered before the Lord.... The priest shall make atonement for them and they shall be forgiven" (4:15). Rulers who sin also incur guilt that may be expiated by the sacrifice of an unblemished male goat (4:22–24). Ordinary folk who sin may bring an unblemished female goat: "You shall lay your hand on the head of the sin offering; and the sin offering shall be slaughtered at the place of the burnt offering.... Thus the priest shall make atonement on your behalf, and you shall be forgiven" (4:29). The high moments of this system of sacrifice occurred at Passover, when the passover lamb was sacrificed and consumed in memory of Yahweh's great act of redeeming Israel from Egyptian slavery and at *yom kippur*, the day of atonement when the high priest entered the temple's most holy place to make atonement for Israel's sin and the scapegoat, the sacrifice that carried the people's sin, was slaughtered outside the walls of Jerusalem.

As we said above, the Letter to the Hebrews draws upon the Hebrew sacrificial system to explain Jesus' atoning work.

The letter also asserts that Jesus' sacrifice supersedes the sacrifices of the old system. Nevertheless, Hebrews clearly interprets Christ's sacrificial death as the means by which human redemption is accomplished:

> But when Christ came as a high priest of the good things that have come, then through the greater and perfect tent (not made with hands, that is, not of this creation), he entered once for all into the Holy Place, not with the blood of goats and calves, but with his own blood, this obtaining eternal redemption. For if the blood of goats and bulls, with the sprinkling of the ashes of a heifer, sanctifies those who have been defiled so that their flesh is purified, how much more will the blood of Christ, who through the eternal Spirit offered himself without blemish to God, purify our conscience from dead works to worship the living God!
>
> (9:11–14)

The word redemption is of crucial significance here. Redemption is made available through Christ's death. To be redeemed is to be bought back. Something needs redemption when it is in some manner "held hostage." Until the final payment has been made on a mortgage—and it has then been redeemed—the mortgaged property does not really belong to its "owner" and can be taken back. A person who must borrow money quickly will sometimes go to a pawnshop and leave an item of security. If he or she repays the loan and repossesses this collateral that person may be said to have *redeemed* the property.

Sin is the great barrier that separates people from God. However, sin not only separates, it also holds people within its power. Paul speaks of sin as holding a power over people. As he puts it we are "of the flesh, sold into slavery under sin," a sin that Paul says "dwells within" us (Rom 7:14b, 20b. Apart from God men and women are captives of sin and held hostage by it. Thankfully, there exists the possibility of escape from sin's power. We can be redeemed because, as Paul says again, we "were bought with a price" (1 Cor 6:20). This price, of course, is the sacrifice Jesus paid "once and for all" on Calvary. Sinfulness is a universal human condition; redemption through Jesus' death a universal possibility.

Since all have sinned and fall short of the glory of God, they are now justified by his grace. It is a gift through the redemption that is in Christ Jesus, whom God put forward as a sacrifice of atonement by his blood, effective through faith. He did this to show his righteousness, because in his divine forbearance he had passed over the sins previously committed; it was to prove at the present time that he himself is righteous and that he justifies the one who has faith in Jesus (Rom 3:23).

The New Testament presents Jesus as the redeemer who in his own person provides the necessary means by which humans escape the power of sin. They can be "bought back," restored to fellowship with God. Restored fellowship with God also means restored fellowship with our fellow human beings. This is why we sing the carol that celebrates, "God and sinners reconciled." Redemption and reconciliation are key ideas that enlarge and amplify the meaning of the comprehensive term salvation.

4.11 The Promised Redeemer

First-century Israel looked forward to the coming of the Messiah, the one who would redeem Israel. To the priestly family of Zechariah and Elizabeth there was born a miraculous baby boy named John. All during Elizabeth's pregnancy Zechariah was mysteriously without the power of speech. After the baby's birth, when he was given the unexpected name of John, Zechariah's tongue was loosed, causing people to wonder what kind of life these extraordinary signs forecast for this child. Zechariah used his newly recovered powers of speech to sing a song that articulated Israel's hope for the promised redeemer and his own belief that John's birth set into motion a train of events that made the coming of Israel's Redeemer a foregone conclusion.

> Blessed be the Lord God of Israel, for he has looked favorably on his people and redeemed them. He has raised up a mighty savior for us in the house of his servant David, as he spoke through the mouth of his holy prophets from of old, that we would be saved from our enemies and from the hand of those who hate us. Thus he has shown the mercy promised to our ancestors, and has remembered his holy covenant, the oath that he swore to our ancestor Abraham, to grant us that we, being rescued from the hands of our enemies, might serve him without fear, in holiness and righteousness before him all our days.
>
> (Luke 1:68–75)

Zechariah's song of celebration for the promised Redeemer's arrival was rooted deep in Israelite history. Israel had long hoped in Yahweh's promise that a Redeemer would come. John Bright illustrates this hope from the prophecy of Isaiah.

> The national hope was retained, but thrust into the future. The promise was not just a promise; it was in

effect a promise to a new and obedient Israel that did not
as yet exist. The national hope thus transmuted and
pushed beyond the existing nation was of such a sort
that it could, and did, survive the fall of the nation, continuing to exist even after the royal theology, which had
created it, had ceased to have meaning. In Isaiah's
preaching there lay the beginning of that restless search
for a pure remnant, a new Israel, one day to rise out of
the fires of tragedy, to which the promises would be
given, and also of the longing for Him who would come
at the issue of history to redeem Israel and establish the
divine rule on earth. This longing, often befooled, found
fulfillment—so Christians say—only when after many a
weary mile there came "in the fullness of time" one "of
the house and lineage of David" who faith hails as "the
Christ, the Son of the Living God."[4]

The gospels tell us that Israel's intense longing for the
promised Redeemer is satisfied in Jesus. New Testament
writers perceive and present Jesus to the world as the longed-
for, long-awaited redeemer, the expected Messiah promised
by God through the prophets who spoke to the divided
monarchies of Israel and Judah. The man we call John the
Baptist explained himself as the one who was preparing the
way for someone greater to follow. Although later John himself would wonder whether Jesus was indeed the Messiah, in
the baptism story John directs the crowd's attention to Jesus,
announcing, "Here is the Lamb of God who takes away the
sin of the world" (John 1:29).

Belief in Jesus as the Messiah of Israel came neither easily
nor without questions. From his prison cell, even John the
Baptist sent some of his followers to Jesus to determine
whether or not Jesus really was the one who had been

promised. Thus they ask him, "Are you the one who is to come, or are we to wait for another?" (Matt 11:3). Even those who were closest to him, Jesus' own disciples, found his redeeming mission difficult to grasp. They did not expect one who would submit to Rome and die on an instrument of shame. After Peter's declaration of faith in Jesus as the Messiah, the Christ of God, Jesus began to teach his disciples the meaning for him and them that he was the promised Messiah. He told them that he must suffer and die. The same Peter who just moments before had proclaimed him that Messiah rebuked Jesus and tried to tell him that the Messiah could not suffer like that.

> From that time Jesus began to show his disciples that he must go to Jerusalem and suffer many things from the elders and chief priests and scribes, and be killed, and on the third day be raised. And Peter took him aside and began to rebuke him, saying, 'God forbid, Lord! This shall never happen to you.' But he turned and said to Peter, 'Get behind me, Satan! You are a stumbling block to me; for you are setting your mind not on divine things but on human.
>
> (Matthew 16:21–23)

Jesus' response is one of the strongest rebukes the Gospels record from his lips: "Get behind me, Satan" (see also Mark 8:27–33), and it is reserved for one who had not understood Jesus' teaching concerning the nature of the redemption he brought.

Even after the crucifixion Jesus' disciples did not clearly perceive that he was the promised Redeemer. Two of his followers, walking the road from Jerusalem to Emmaus, meet a stranger who asks them what they are discussing. They are amazed that anyone can be ignorant of the events that have rocked Jerusalem for the last week. They tell the stranger about Jesus of Nazareth, "who was a prophet mighty in deed and word before God and all the people, and how our chief priests and leaders handed him over to be condemned to death and crucified him. *But we had hoped that he was the one who was to redeem Israel"* (Luke 24:19–21, emphasis added). Finally their eyes will be opened, and yet, even after the crucifixion and resurrection they did not see.

The church and individual followers of Jesus are not immune to the disciples' misperception. We all possess a strong tendency to make Jesus over into our image, and therefore we dare not lose sight of the important Pauline phrase, "the Christ of God." At the center of the question of Jesus' identity we find the suffering redeemer. Jesus not only redeemed us through suffering and death, he invites those who would follow him to live as he lived. The Jews of the New Testament era were looking for a war hero, someone who would gather an army and drive the Romans out of Palestine and reestablish David's throne in Jerusalem. Today's Christians still seem to be looking for a war hero, a God who will drive out by overwhelming force whatever personification of evil we see. John V. Taylor sheds an important ray of light on this tendency:

> We human beings are physically puny in a world of brute force. We admire the strongest, the victor.... So, with our gift for fantasy, we project those images of domination out into the skies and call it God.... God (unlike us) can do exactly as God wants at any moment. God (like our secret wishes) fixes everything. Get him on you side and you can't lose.... If Jesus is Lord in that sense then the thirty years of Incarnation were like an

exceptional assignment he had to undertake involving a disguise and some temporary hardship and humiliation.... And the victim on the cross was enduring merely the last bad patch before the climax when he could throw off his disguise, mission accomplished, and get back on the throne of the universe. The helplessness and pain tell us nothing new about God.

That is how the church has too often presented the story.[5]

If we take seriously the biblical saying that Jesus is the express image of God, a saying that allows us to infer that God's action in the world will conform to the action disclosed in the life of Jesus, we will need to alter accordingly our understanding of what God is doing in the world. No longer will we allow ourselves to look for a heavenly king on a warhorse. We will instead need to look for a king riding on a donkey, facing the worst that evil can do and yet refusing to use the weapons of evil to fight it. Here we find a king who forgave his worst enemies and taught us to overcome ours by loving them.

This heavenly king engages human life at its points of greatest suffering and then endures. This king overcomes evil not with force of arms but with good. This king turns the other cheek, goes the second mile, prays for those who harm others, and repays evil with God's true power, the power of love. "By this," Jesus says, "will everyone know you are my disciples, that you have such love for one another" (John 13:35). The apostle Paul refers to this love as that which "bears all things, believes all things, hopes all things, endures all things" (1 Cor 13:7).

God brought redemption to the world in a way quite different than humans would have planned it. That is but one indication that it is God's doing.

4.12 The Meaning of Jesus' Redemption

If to know Jesus means to know God, then it seems to follow that Jesus' mission would also be God's mission. If, through Jesus Christ, we are God's redeemed people then we are called to live as God would have us live. That means Jesus' mission is also our mission. Therefore we might expect to find that redeemed people will see their lives according to a perspective that their unredeemed neighbors do not share. Furthermore, this different perspective on their lives will result in a lifestyle for the redeemed that differs from that of their unredeemed neighbors. In this light Christ's redemption serves a very practical aspect in our lives. News headlines like the following two are common occurrences.

> **Armed Gunman Opens Fire in Local Restaurant Leaving Two Dead and Several Wounded**

> **Couple Abandon Two Children in Chicago Northside Apartment While They Gamble in Las Vegas for the Weekend**

Understood theologically, these headlines might read as follows:

> **Local Man Sins Leaving
> Two Dead, Several Wounded
> and Countless Lives in
> Confusion and Pain**

> **Sinful Behavior Leads Couple to
> Abandon Two Children in
> Neighborhood Apartment. But the
> Damage of Sinful Action Surrounds
> Us on Every Side**

That American society has come to excuse wrongful action as a behavioral problem for which perpetrators are finally not responsible is now a commonplace observation. In a "no-fault" culture, solutions often take the form of therapy. When the human predicament is understood as anxiety, then its remedies will come from the world of medicine and therapy. However, the Bible understands the human predicament to be sin, and it judges wrong action as moral failure. Such an assessment means that we are dealing with something more serious than anxiety; from the Bible's point of view we must deal with guilt.

The Bible tells the story of a God who first created humans to be in fellowship with him. The story of the Garden of Eden helps us understand the loving creation and the freedom God meant for us. Genesis paints a lovely picture of the world that

God created and always intended to be. More importantly, this narrative recounts the ideal relationship that God desired with creation, especially with humanity. This relationship can only be described as an intimacy that enabled humans to walk with "the Lord God as he was walking in the garden in the cool of the day" (Gen 3:8). Genesis portrays the divine-human relationship as intimate and free, but not without limits. The forbidden tree of the knowledge of good and evil offered humans a choice. They could obey the Lord God's command, but they were also free to disobey. Disobedience severs fellowship with the Creator. Submission to evil (in the Garden story represented by the serpent) gives evil power over us and severs our relationship with God, destroying the divine-human intimacy in the process. Tragically, by their own free choice, humans come under the bondage of sin. They must remain in sin's power unless and until a redeemer buys them back.

The Old Testament unflinchingly tells the story of people whom God constantly calls and redeems yet who continue to fall in spite of the loving offers of the Redeemer God. The relationship between God and humankind becomes troubled, full of alienation, disobedience, and falsehood. It becomes a story of retribution and heartache even as it continues to be a story of reconciliation and redemption. While God is often angry and even repents of the act of creating humans, ("The Lord was grieved that he had made man on the earth, and his heart was filled with pain" [Gen 6:6]) God never completely abandons creation.

We are told the story of a God who became angry enough to destroy humankind:

> The Lord saw that the wickedness of humankind was great in the earth, and that every inclination of the thoughts of their hearts was only evil continually. And the Lord was sorry that he had made humankind on the earth, and it grieved him to his heart. So the Lord said, "I will blot out from the earth the human beings I have created—people together with animals and creeping things and birds of the air, for I am sorry that I have made them."
>
> (Genesis 6:5–7)

In this narrative it is the complete wickedness of the people that angers God. They had surrendered to evil; "every inclination of the thoughts of [the human] heart was only evil all the time" (Gen 6:5). The Bible shows Yahweh to be a God who must deal with a difficult dilemma. Yahweh is the Creator-God who loves creation. At the same time, Yahweh despises the evil and injustice that now reside in and enslave that creation. God's beloved creation, and the darlings of it, humans created in God's own image, continually give themselves over to evil. What is a loving God to do? God must uphold the divine standards of good (which we call righteousness or holiness). Yet God will not surrender divine love for the creature. The divine answer is to redeem, to buy back those who have fallen into the clutches of sin and evil.

Luke 7 tells the story of Jesus' visit to the home of Simon the Pharisee. Simon had invited Jesus to dinner. At some point during the evening a woman of the city whom the text describes as a "known sinner" entered the house and took a position behind the couch where Jesus reclined at the meal. "She stood behind him at his feet, weeping, and began to bathe his feet with her tears and to dry them with her hair. Then she continued kissing his feet and anointing them with the ointment" [that she had brought with her].

The members of the dinner party watched in amazed shock. How would Jesus react? Apparently he looked upon her kindly, for Simon finally objected. " 'If you knew what kind of woman was touching you,' he said, 'you wouldn't let her near you.' " Jesus rebuked his host and then stunned every onlooker in the room when he told the woman that her sins were forgiven and urged her not to return to her sinful life. Jesus reached out to a woman whom the religious people of his day judged to be beyond redemption. The redemption made available to us in Jesus will shock our sensibilities as well. This redemption insists upon a redeemed lifestyle:

> Now this I affirm and insist on in the Lord: you must no longer live as the Gentiles live, in the futility of their minds. They are darkened in their understanding, alienated from the life of God because of their ignorance and hardness of heart. They have lost all sensitivity and have abandoned themselves to licentiousness, greedy to practice every kind of impurity. That is not the way you learned Christ! For surely you have heard about him and were taught in him, as truth is in Jesus. You were taught to put away your former way of life, your old self, corrupt and deluded by its lusts, and to be renewed in the spirit of your minds, and to clothe yourselves with the new self, created according to the likeness of God in true righteousness and holiness.
>
> (Ephesians 4:17–24)

To be redeemed is to be bought back. The result of this purchase is that humans are free to be restored into right relationship with God. Reconciliation with God is the foremost consequence of redemption; it achieves the intent of the first and greatest commandment of Torah. But this changed relationship also has moral consequences. An imperative follows the indicative. Free from the clutches of sin, followers of Jesus may now follow the second commandment too, the one that points us toward right relationship with our neighbors. We are to love them even as we love ourselves.

4.2 Jesus and Revelation

Christians say that in Jesus of Nazareth the fullness of God is revealed. The fourteenth chapter of John recounts a conversation between Jesus and his disciples. Jesus has just said that he is about to leave them to prepare a place for them. Thomas, full of fear, worries that they will not be able to find Jesus in this new place since they do not know the way. Then Jesus replies, "I am the way, the truth, and the life. No one comes to the Father except through me. If you know me, you will know my Father also. From now on you do know him and have seen him." For some reason Philip does not grasp the point and says, "Lord, show us the Father and we will be satisfied." To this demand Jesus replies,

> Whoever has seen me has seen the Father. How can you say, "Show us the Father"? Do you not believe that I am in the Father and the Father is in me? The words that I say to you I do not say on my own; but the Father who dwells in me does his works. Believe me that I am in the Father and the Father is in me; but if you do not, then believe me because of the works themselves.
>
> (John 14:1:11)

Such stories and statements underwrite the Christian confession that Jesus is God's self-disclosure, that is, God's revelation to us.

The stories of Jesus are the most precious of biblical resources. These stories picture Jesus for us: Jesus who walks and talks at equal ease with commoners and with the elite; Jesus who, even when weary, has compassion on those who wish to hear him; Jesus who cares for Samaritans and Romans as well as Jews; Jesus who confronts oppression, especially oppression in the name of religion or God; Jesus who gives the blessings and warnings of the beatitudes. All these pictures—and more—of Jesus leap from the stories in the Gospels. These pictures not only *tell us* about Jesus, the New Testament consistently claims that they *show us* God.

The daily experience of walking in Jesus' presence later took the form of story. In the oral tradition the stories about Jesus were recast as the theological statements of the New Testament epistles. For example, John's gospel contains the story of Jesus' teachings in his conversation with Phillip. That conversation includes this declaration—"He who has seen me has seen the Father." The letter to the Colossians turns this declaration and the narrative events surrounding it into the following theological proposition—a central dogma of the church about the nature of Jesus:

> He is the image of the invisible God, the firstborn of all creation; for in him all things in heaven and on earth were created, things visible and things invisible—all things have been created through him and for him.... For in him all the fullness of God was pleased to dwell, and through him God was pleased to reconcile to himself all things, whether on earth or in heaven, by making peace through the blood of his cross.
>
> (Colossians 1:15–20, passim)

Jesus reveals God. We understand the incarnation as God in human form. Jesus is God who can be seen with the eye, heard with the ear, and touched with the hand. In Jesus God connects with humanity and humanity connects with God.

God takes into the divine being the pain and sorrow, the joys and triumphs of creation. In Jesus, the infinite God identifies fully with the plight of humankind, the finite. In the incarnation Jesus reveals to us the heart of God that desires only the peace and well-being, the *shalom,* of all creation.

The church, the people of God look to Jesus as savior, lord, judge, and God. As Albert Nolan put it,

> Jesus cannot be fully identified with that great religious phenomenon of the western world known as Christianity. He was much more than the founder of one of the world's great religions. He stands above Christianity as the judge of all it has done in his name. Nor can historical Christianity claim him as its exclusive possession. Jesus belongs to all.[6]

4.21 The God Whom Jesus Reveals

What does it mean to say that "in Christ the fullness of God dwelt bodily"? Colossians is not the only New Testament letter that employs the most exalted language to describe the nature of Christ and his relationship to God (a theological sub-discipline called "Christology"). Philippians 2:5–11 also helps us to perceive the nature of Christ and thus see into the very heart of God. Colossians tells us that God makes peace through the blood of Christ's cross, an idea that this letter shares with Philippians 2.

We need to know a bit of background in order to interpret this beautiful passage. Philippi was a Roman colony. As the Roman armies advanced across the Mediterranean basin, they sometimes destroyed whole cities where the population resisted too strongly. Then the Roman government would plant a colony on the site of the destroyed city. Such was the case in Philippi, where a city had existed for many centuries prior to the coming of the Romans. As a Roman colony, Philippi's population contained a higher than average percentage of Roman citizens. These people were very proud of their citizenship, which conferred social and legal privileges not enjoyed by the common folk. Thus the sentence, "I am a Roman," claimed a privileged status more than it may have identified a person's ethnicity. Roman citizens were proud of their citizenship, and it showed in their haughtiness and arrogant bearing. They were society's upper crust and they behaved like it.

Of course, some of these Roman citizens were converted to Christianity at Philippi. To the church there Paul later wrote, "Our citizenship is in heaven" (Phil 3:20). One would think that Paul was prouder by far of that citizenship than his status as a citizen of Rome, and that he hoped the Philippian converts would share in the same pride. To take pride in heavenly citizenship is to swear allegiance to a heavenly king absolutely different in character and governance from the Emperor in Rome. Paul's picture of the heavenly king stands the Roman notion of royal power on its head:

> Let this same mind be in you that was in Christ Jesus, who, though he was in the form of God, did not regard equality with God as something to be exploited, but emptied himself, taking the form of a slave, being born in human likeness. And being found in human form, he humbled himself and became obedient to the point of death—even death on a cross. Therefore God also highly exalted him and gave him the name that is above every name, so that at the name of Jesus every knee should bend, in heaven and on earth and under the earth,

and every tongue should confess that Jesus Christ is
Lord to the glory of God the Father

(Philippians 2:5–11)

The idea is further developed in the Colossians text. We all
know of rulers who say, "Let there be peace between us. I
will make you pay the price of reconciliation." The God
revealed in Jesus Christ also says, "Let there be peace
between us. Let me be reconciled to you." Unlike the rulers
of this world, however, the God revealed in Jesus says, "I will
pay the price of reconciliation. I will make peace through the
humbling of myself as I take on human form and take up the
way of the cross." Every knee will bow to this God revealed
in Christ, but not because God has taken hold of people by
the scruff of the neck and forced them to their knees. Rather,
people will spontaneously fall worshiping to their knees as
they are brought face to face with the holy and divine love
that in its sheer, transcendent goodness offered itself for us.

4.3 Jesus and Discipleship

From the gospel narratives it appears that Jesus enjoyed
wide popularity among the people who lived in and around
his home district of Galilee. Many people followed him, listening to his teaching and observing the miracles he per-
formed. From this large group he selected a smaller circle of
close followers who became his disciples. Luke 6 carries the
account of Jesus' selection of "The Twelve" who by this
selection became apostles, "appointed representatives." That
they numbered twelve is likely no accident; the number must
have been meant to symbolically represent the twelve tribes
of Israel. Although of this group we tend to interchange disciple and apostle, in point of fact, the number of Jesus' disci-

ples was much larger. Anyone who chose to follow him and accept his easy yoke could be a disciple. So, for example, from this group the Seventy were appointed to preach the good news in the surrounding towns and villages (see also Luke 10:1–16; Matt 9:37–38; 10:1–16). Although contemporary followers of Jesus may be commissioned as apostles, it is certainly true that we all are privileged to become Jesus' followers, his disciples.

Disciples are those who accept the discipline of another, their teacher or *rabbi*. Jesus was often referred to by this honorable title. It was common for rabbis of Jesus' day to surround themselves with a small circle of students who were understood to be disciples of the rabbi. Jesus invited any who would follow him to take his yoke upon them and learn from him, saying that his yoke—the discipline of his teaching—is easy and the burden of learning from him is light (see Matt 11:29–30). Nevertheless, Jesus also warned those who consider following after him that such discipleship has very serious consequences:

> Then Jesus told his disciples, "'If any want to become my followers, let them deny themselves and take up their cross and follow me. For those who want to save their life will lose it, and those who lose their life for my sake will find it. For what will it profit them if they gain the whole world but forfeit their life? Or what will they give in return for their life?"
>
> (Matthew 16:24–26)

Jesus' Sermon on the Mount (Matt 5—7) is the core of his instruction to those who intend to be his disciples. We frequently cite the Great Commission of Matthew 28:19–20, where Jesus commands the remaining apostles to go and make disciples. To be a disciple is more than simply being converted to Christ. Conversion *begins* discipleship. The resurrected Lord commands his followers to baptize and to teach converts all that he has commanded.

In the context of Matthew's gospel, one naturally will refer back to the Sermon on the Mount as the law of Christ to be obeyed by those who would be his disciples. However, the Sermon contains some of Jesus' most difficult sayings and teachings. There we find the sayings that elevate Christian discipleship to a standard even higher than Torah: Jesus' disciples will not utter harsh words against those with whom they disagree, in fact they will practice face to face forgiveness and reconciliation; Jesus' followers will not cast a lustful glance; Jesus' followers will love their enemies; Jesus' followers will be content to practice their piety in secret and without public acclaim. These commands, and the balance of the Sermon, raise Christian discipleship to a very high standard. We should not expect that such discipleship will be easy.

Following Jesus in Christian discipleship is more than loyalty to an ideal or a set of principles. Christian discipleship is loyalty to a person, the person of the resurrected Lord. Jesus did not walk the earth easily during his public ministry. Given the character of his experience, perhaps we ought to consider the possibility that loyalty to him will cost us something too. To know the risen Christ is at least a two-fold process. Our experience with the resurrected Jesus chastens us, redeems, comforts, and heals us. Through the gospels we come to see the manner of his earthly life and teaching. This knowledge provides us with a framework for interpreting our experience.

The resurrected Lord who saves is the Jesus of the Bible. We don't know everything about him. In fact we don't know some of the basic information a modern biographer would be sure to establish. What we have are the stories told by those who followed him, who were encountered by him after the resurrection, and those to whom they told their story, in a word, their testimony.

If we would know who Jesus is so that we might glimpse who God is, we will engage the stories of the Gospels. They are formative for us as individual disciples and, collectively, as the church. They teach us who Jesus is, what Jesus understood as important, how Jesus lived, and how Jesus' followers must live if they dare call themselves his disciples.

The Jesus who walked dusty roads turning aside to engage people engages us through those same stories as the Holy Spirit imprints them in our hearts. In the stories Jesus comes alive. He is flexible and tough-minded. He gets tired and angry. He teaches and urges his disciples on even as he prepares them for his physical absence. Jesus is more than a mushy, sentimental idea we can call upon to support our own biases. The Jesus of history lived dangerously, challenging both religious and political authority in a quest for divine justice on behalf of the poor and the outcast. This is the Jesus we wish to know. This is the Jesus who calls us to follow.

4.4 *Excursus:* Jesus and Implications for the Church's Teachers

The central teaching task of the church is introducing people to Jesus and helping them to come to know him and who he is. In this sense, the church is called to the basic role of teaching people to be followers of Jesus. Faithfulness in this endeavor requires, first, a personal allegiance to Jesus; second, the calling and gifts of the teacher; third, the development of these gifts; and, fourth, a basic knowledge of the

Jesus presented through scripture and as understood by the church.

The Church of God, Anderson, Indiana, has long understood that a saving experience with Jesus through the Holy
Spirit provides entry into the church. This experience is our
introduction to Jesus. Our understanding of who Jesus is
grows over our whole lifetime, as we experience his compan-
ionship. Therefore, the educational ministries of the church
should be directed to the life span of its people, not focused
on children, youth, or adults only; and directed from the distinctive perspective of the Church of God as it addresses the
primary themes of unity, holiness, and healing.

The Bible is available to us in many translations. Short of
studying scripture in its original languages, study in several
translations helps to open the pages of scripture to teachers
and students alike. Curricular resources help teachers prepare
and include background information about the biblical text
and the church's understanding across the years. Therefore,
attention should be paid to a plan, a curriculum, that
addresses the whole Bible and all of its major themes—not
only select passages that support doctrinal positions.

Look for curricular resources that include a serious
approach to the Bible. Indications that a curriculum takes the
Bible seriously: (1) The lesson is planned around the biblical
material—the biblical material isn't merely coincidentally
attached. (2) The biblical material occupies a significant
amount of classroom time. (3) Resources presented to the
teacher are prepared by persons gifted in biblical interpretation. (4) The curriculum provides helps for the teacher that
engage class members with the biblical narrative.

With attention to our personal relationships with God, with
a continued commitment to our personal learning and study
of the Bible, and with the undergirding of the Holy Spirit as

we approach the teaching task, we can grow in our relationship and knowledge of the Lord Jesus Christ. We and those we teach will come more and more to know who he is and to allow him to reform and reshape our lives in his image.

God seeks a people whose relationship to him and to others is based on love. The picture of our redeemer that we present to those we teach needs to reflect both the sacrifice Jesus made on our behalf on the cross and the glory of the resurrected Lord in an empty tomb. This Jesus shows us God and calls us into God's service, to join in redeeming activity, and ultimately to share in victorious celebration. Therefore, our teaching will always call students beyond themselves to an engagement with the world in which they live and work, guided by the understanding that they are to continue the redemption of the world, empowered by the continuing presence of the Holy Spirit.

For the called, gifted, and faithful teacher the opportunity to become involved in the lives of students is the reward. They learn, they grow, they struggle, and, at times, they suffer. We share their pain even as we are there when the "lights go on" in their lives. Therefore, our teaching is ultimately relational. The teacher and the curriculum serve as bridges between God and persons and between persons and persons. Each lesson and each classroom experience should be directed toward an encounter between God and persons so that each student will, as did our Lord, grow "in wisdom and stature and favor with God" and others.

A great temptation for any teacher is to create yet another picture of Jesus, one that arises out of personal life experiences. A better approach invites those who teach to immerse themselves in the stories of Jesus, the teachings of the church about Jesus, and the inspiration and guidance of the Holy

Spirit. Engaging those stories with an open and seeking mind and heart will transform both lives and teaching. By immersing ourselves in the Gospels we develop our personal images of God. The more these images are formed by scripture, the more faithful they become. One of the great joys of teaching comes as we watch these stories take root and grow in our lives and the lives of those we teach. The one who would teach others about Jesus will want to read and reread the Gospels. They are the primary written source of our knowledge of the Jesus we love and proclaim.

Notes

1. Ernst Kasemann, *Jesus Means Freedom,* trans by Frank Clark (Philadelphia: Fortress, 1969) 146.

2. John Bright *The Kingdom of God* (Nashville: Abingdon-Cokesbury, 1953), 230.

3. A reference to the tabernacle in which Israel worshiped Yahweh during their journey through the wilderness.

4. John Bright, *The History of Israel* (Philadelphia: Westminster Press, 1959) 297–298.

5. John V. Taylor, *Weep Not for Me: Meditations on the Cross and Resurrection* (Geneva, Switzerland: World Council of Churches, 1986), 7–8.

6. Albert Nolan, *Jesus before Christianity* (Maryknoll: Orbis Books, 1976), 3.

Chapter Five

The Church

—Richard Willowby—

Now when Jesus came into the district of Caesarea Philippi, he asked his disciples, "Who do people say that the Son of Man is?" And they said, "Some say John the Baptist, but others Elijah, and still others Jeremiah or one of the prophets." He said to them, "But who do you say that I am?" Simon Peter answered, "You are the Messiah, the Son of the living God." And Jesus answered him, "Blessed are you, Simon son of Jonah! For flesh and blood has not revealed this to you, but my Father in heaven. And I tell you, you are Peter, and on this rock I will build my church, and the gates of Hades will not prevail against it. I will give you the keys of the kingdom of heaven, and whatever you bind on earth will be bound in heaven, and whatever you loose on earth will be loosed in heaven."

Matthew 16:13–19 (NRSV)

5.0 Introduction

Church people often struggle with what seems to them a canyon-size gap between what they believe the church ought to be and what it appears to actually be. The church of our day struggles seriously with the world and with itself, trying to come to terms with its own mission and the best ways in which to express that mission. This struggle takes place within an ever-changing environment that reshapes the church as well. American Catholics and Protestants alike feel uneasy in the face of such sweeping change. Some years ago, *Time* quoted an elderly Catholic woman from Iowa as saying, "Well, I hope that I die soon so that I can die a Catholic!" Her sentiments on the sweeping changes within her church would find parallel echoes in many Protestant hearts.

One important way to address the many issues facing the church is to build up a theological understanding of the church. This understanding begins in the Bible. Here the record of the birth of the church is found as well as descriptions of its nature and prescriptions for its work. We learn the mission of the church—its reason for being—in the narratives and letters of the New Testament. We even find there a deep connection between the church and Israel, a connection that also shapes the practices and the very nature of the Christian community.

Christians increasingly are coming to appreciate this connection. As one illustration of many we might cite the growing number of congregations that schedule the educational experience of a Passover meal during Holy Week. Such experiences enlarge their understanding of New Testament teaching concerning Christ's sacrificial death.

The New Testament, especially the Letter to the Hebrews, draws extensively on the meaning of Passover and the

Hebrew sacrificial system. One might go so far as to say that one cannot read Hebrews very well without some prior knowledge of first-century Jewish temple religion. A connection exists between Israel, the old people of God, and the church, the new people of God. As careful students of the New Testament vision of the church, we must be ready to explore this connection and others for the light they shed on our theological task.

The purpose of this chapter, then, is to explore a theology of the church within the perspective of the biblical record and to consider the implications of such a theology for the teachers whose work is a crucial aspect of the ministry of discipleship in the local congregation.

5.01 Viewing the Church and Its Teachers Historically and Theologically

Prior to the sixteenth century, Christendom was divided west and east into the Catholic and Orthodox churches, respectively. The sixteenth-century Reformation initially produced the so-called "magisterial" churches—Lutheran, Reformed, and Anglican. It also spawned the numerous churches of the Radical Reformation—Mennonites, Brethren, German Baptists, and others. Differences in social and economic class as well as matters of theology account for the eventual creation of hundreds of different Christian church groups.

For centuries European Christians, other than those of the Radical Reformation, contested one another for the right to call themselves the true church. Since the church in Europe was legally and socially intertwined with the state, any nation could have but one church. Rivals and critics of the established church did not enjoy the same legal protection that European governments gave to the official church. Instead, these protest groups were often considered sectarian and given a decidedly second-class status. The great sixteenth century reformer Martin Luther even stooped so low as to label peace-loving Mennonites *schwärmer,* an uncomplimentary German word that in a twentieth century idiom might be colloquially translated "Holy Roller."

The ratification of the US Constitution and its famous disestablishment clause forced American Christianity to work out very different understandings about church organization. The European division of church and sect did not fit an American context where no church enjoyed governmental support. The solution was the creation of the distinctively American expression of organized Christianity, the denomination. Neither officially established church nor sectarian protest group, the American denomination was a voluntary group that survived and expanded as it attracted new members to its fold. This situation could make for an excessive denominational loyalty as well as considerable competition for members. That is precisely the situation that developed in the United States after 1840.

During the same time period some Christians grew increasingly concerned for this competitiveness and the fragmentation that they believed was its cause. D. S. Warner was one such person, and the movement known as the Church of God (Anderson, Indiana) grew out of his vision, and that of a few others, of the church beyond such denominational division.

Warner was not alone in his pursuit of such a church. Earlier in the century Alexander Campbell and Barton W. Stone had launched a restorationist movement determined to practice—exclusive of all else—the teachings of the New

Testament and to be known as "Christians only." Eventually this movement led to the formation of the Church of Christ, the Independent Christian Churches, and the Christian Church (Disciples).

Another person who shared convictions about the church resembling the Campbell-Stone group was a German Reformed minister and evangelist named John Winebrenner. Around his work another group also came into being, the General Eldership of the Churches of God of North America. While affirming that unity is God's gift to all Christians, each of these reformers earnestly believed that the church could be a visible, recognizable witness to the spiritual gift of Christian unity.

D. S. Warner grew up in a home that cared little for Christianity or the church. However, as a young man he was converted in a revival meeting conducted by members of the Winebrenner group. In that context he soon experienced a call to the ministry and served as a duly licensed evangelist and home missionary of the General Eldership. Through the lens of that group Warner's theological vision of the church began to grow. To that group's vision he later added the Holiness Movement's teaching on entire sanctification, concluding that the sanctifying work of the Holy Spirit gives Christians the divine love that serves to unify the church in the "bond of perfectness."

Warner found other denominations, organizations, and church groups resistant to his vision. So he struck out on his own in company with a few like-minded souls, and the Church of God movement was born. Almost two centuries have passed since the earliest of these visionaries saw the possibility of real Christian unity expressed in the visible church. We have yet to see the fulfillment of their vision, yet the movements formed in the wake of their lives continue to strive for the unity of all believers and work to eliminate barriers between Christians.

Such movements also shape the way in which their people read and interpret the New Testament passages on the church. Early Church of God people often spoke of "seeing the church." By this they meant their vision of the "New Testament church," a church beyond denominational limitations. They believed that this church stretched across time and space, manifesting itself as a faithful force determined to live out God's will in daily life and to witness to the reality of the kingdom of God now present in the hearts and lives of people. They believed this vision to be the result of the illuminating activity of the Holy Spirit.

This vision of the church provides a context for our individual roles as Christians and as teachers. Even as he invited the Twelve into fellowship with him, so Jesus invites all persons to become members of his body, the church. Teachers share in the church's fundamental task—to follow the Great Commission of Matthew 28:19-20: "make disciples of all nations, baptizing them in the name of the Father and of the Son and of the Holy Spirit, and teaching them to obey everything that I have commanded you." As they work at their ministry of helping people to Christian maturity in obedience to all that Jesus taught, teachers at the same time enable those people to become effective members of the local congregation. In this, today's teachers follow in the footsteps of the Master, who was known respectfully by his students as "Rabbi." The church's teachers are called to kindle and nourish a fire in the hearts of their students that will energize their growth into a discipleship of such character that they will live faithfully in relationship with the Jesus whose body the church is.

God does not save us merely for our own benefit. As people are saved, God joins them to the church. New Testament writers describe Jesus' love for the church in the passionate terms of a marriage embrace. He loves the church as a bridegroom loves his bride. Jesus' sacrificial death must be understood to have accomplished more than the salvation of individuals who are then free to live disconnected from other radically individual souls. Instead we must think of Jesus' death as purchasing salvation that also and at the same time creates the church. Jesus went to Golgotha for all those souls whose salvation taken together compose the church. The church is worth death for Jesus; it is his own pearl of great price.

> Christ loved the church and gave himself up for her ... to make her holy by cleansing her with the washing of water by the word ... to present the church to himself in splendor, without a spot or wrinkle or anything of the kind—yes, so that she may be holy and without blemish.
>
> (Ephesians 5:25–27)

The saving work of Christ brings individual men and women from varied backgrounds into the community called church. James Massey highlights the special character of this community. "The major New Testament terms are brother, sister, friend, and occasionally neighbor. The closeness of Christian relations is akin to that of persons born from the same womb. All true believers are children in the same family." God's saving work restores human relationships. From the very beginning of creation God has called men and women into relationship with God and with each other. Sin ruptured the intimate relationship between God and humanity and between humans. Nevertheless God provided the means to restore people to wholeness and in that restoration make possible true intimacy with God and with our fellow human beings. The church is the community of such restored relationships.

The Ten Commandments, for example, articulate God's intentions for divine-human and human-human relations. The first four commandments, the so-called "First Table," define the relationship between Yahweh and Israel and, by extension, between God and the people of God everywhere. The six remaining commandments of the "Second Table" prescribe normative relationships between human beings. God desires that the church described in the New Testament be the ultimate expression of the same kind of healed and restored community articulated in the Ten Commandments. The New Testament's dominant metaphor to express this community refers to the church as the body of Christ. This spiritual truth is at the heart of any discussion of the church. It revolutionizes our thinking and our living if we are but able to hear it:

> For just as the body is one and has many members, and all the members of the body, though many, are one body, so it is with Christ. For in the one Spirit we were all baptized into one body—Jews or Greeks, slaves or free, and we were all made to drink of one Spirit. Indeed, the body does not consist of one member but of many.
>
> (1 Corinthians 12:12–14)

The church is the body of Christ, working to fulfill his purposes in the world as it witnesses to the present reality of the rule and reign of God—in a word, the kingdom. Through the animating activity of the Holy Spirit, Christ is present in the world through the church. God enables the ministries of the church through the gifts of the Spirit. These gifts equip individual members of Christ's body for their own special places of service and, as such, are given for the strengthening of all.

Teaching is one such gift that strengthens the entire body. This gift, perhaps more than any other, directs and propels the members of the body toward Christian maturity. This maturity is essential if the church is to be a faithful witness in the world. The only way in which the world can recognize itself to be the world and not the church is for the church's witness to be faithful and healthy. When that witness lacks faithfulness, the body becomes unhealthy. When the body becomes unhealthy, it acts in ways that ultimately confuse the world. A confused world finds it easy to turn its eyes away from the Christ toward whom the body must ultimately point if it is to be faithful to him. The body of Christ, in large measure, depends upon a disciplined and dedicated teaching ministry for its health and for the faithfulness of its witness.

The church is the means of hope, then, for the individual and for the world. The church is guaranteed by the blood of Jesus and will always exist, not necessarily in the forms and structures with which we are most familiar, but always nevertheless. There will always be some who respond to Christ's call and who, in Christ, become part of his body.

> Faith in the indestructibility of the church … is related
> primarily to the whole church as a believing community.
> It is not primarily related to certain ecclesiastical institu-
> tions or authorities.[1]

Finally, then, the vision of the church that we put forward here argues for freedom from the individualistic limits of our own narrow and private worlds. The new thing that God is doing in the world escapes the complete grasp of even the most vivid imagination. God's work exceeds the limits of any one congregation and any one church group or movement. Nevertheless, to be saved is to be grafted into Christ's body.

Christian discipleship necessarily entails membership in *some* group that is the visible manifestation of Christ's body, in other words, some local congregation of the church. *Knowing that we belong to all of God's people for all time does not eliminate the need to belong to a specific congregation.* If our membership in the Christian community called church is to have any meaning at all, then we must say that as we belong to Christ, so we belong to each other.

5.1 The New Testament and the Resurrection

The New Testament exists because the first Christians believed in the resurrection of Jesus from the dead. Indeed, the gospels and Acts, the letters and the Book of Revelation all, in one way or another bear witness to Jesus' life, death, and resurrection. Written in the light of the resurrection, the gospels seek to inform and persuade nonbelievers that Jesus is the Christ. As the Gospel according to John says,

> Now Jesus did many other signs in the presence of his disciples, which are not recorded in this book. But these are written so that you may come to believe that Jesus is the Messiah, the Son of God, and that through believing you might have life in his name.
>
> (John 20:30–31)

Saul of Tarsus, encountered by the risen Lord on the Damascus road, experienced a radical transformation. Once a "ravager of the church" Saul became Paul the Apostle, whose witness to the resurrection in Asia and Europe greatly expanded the first-century church. His letters to many of these churches treat matters that would not have arisen had people not believed that Jesus was raised from the dead. At the very conclusion of the New Testament the Book of Revelation anticipates the return of the resurrected Lord to gather up the church. The resurrection of Jesus is the center of the New Testament.

Only a moment's reflection is necessary to see that Jesus' resurrection bears the same importance to the New Testament as the Exodus does to the Old. Even as the Exodus gives birth to the people of God named Israel, the resurrection gives birth to the people of God named the church. Just as Israel interpreted the meaning and purpose of its existence through the Exodus, so Jesus' resurrection sheds light on the meaning and purpose of the church. It was to the resurrection that the first Christian missionaries witnessed as they spread across the Mediterranean basin. They called on the pagan peoples of the Roman Empire to be grafted into Christ and made joint heirs to the resurrection. Those who responded to that call became members of the Christian communities called "churches" (*ecclesia* in New Testament Greek). There they were instructed and encouraged in the ethical consequences that followed upon entrance into the life of the resurrection. As Paul frequently exhorted his congregations,

> So if you have been raised with Christ, seek the things that are above, where Christ is, seated at the right hand of God. Set your mind on the things that are above, not on the things that are on earth, for you have died, and your life is hidden with Christ in God.
>
> (Colossians 3:1–3)

The arena of this ethical encouragement and instruction is the church, the community of the crucified and resurrected Lord.

5.21 The Church and Redemption

If the church is the community of the crucified and resurrected Lord, then the redemption purchased by that crucifixion and resurrection is the gateway to the church. Redemption, conversion, regeneration (to be born again), justification, and salvation are a cluster of related words that touch on aspects of the needed reconciliation with God made possible through faith in Jesus.

• **Redemption** means to be "bought back," and refers to a person's release from the power of sin to return to God. To be converted means to have reversed directions. Before conversion the direction of a person's life faces away from God; after conversion the person has made an about face to live life facing toward God. The experience of regeneration refers to Jesus' statement to Nicodemus (see John 3:1–21); the term signifies the "new creature in Christ" that we become, the work of salvation that God does in us. Justification is a technical Pauline theological term that refers to what God does for us. To be justified is to have our relationship with God restored. Salvation is the comprehensive term that connects all of these aspects. The two accepted definitions of the Greek word *sodzo* (which the English Bible translates as "save") are (1) to rescue from imminent danger and (2) to make whole.

Taken together, all of these terms are aspects of the life of a person who has been both rescued and made whole by the power of God manifest in Christ Jesus. When we speak of the church as the community of redemption, we refer to all of those who testify to this power and who can say with the Apostle Paul, "It is no longer I who live, but it is Christ who lives in me. And the life I now live in the flesh I live by faith in the Son of God, who loved me and gave himself for me" (Gal 2:20).

• **Sin**, *hamartia* in New Testament Greek, means to miss the mark, to fall short of God's ideal for human existence. We miss the mark both in our fundamental being and in our day-to-day actions. This falling short has disastrous consequences, for sin alienates us from our fellow human beings and from God. This broken relationship with God leaves us without God and without hope in the world. From the New Testament's perspective, people can be divided into two groups: sinners and redeemed. Sinners are, in a word, lost. The redeemed have, as in the case of the prodigal son, come to themselves and realized their danger. They have been rescued and made whole. They are saved. Their human relationships are restored as is their relationship with God. The saved are no longer alienated from God but are "joint heirs with Christ" (Rom 8:15–17).

Salvation restores us to God and places us in the body of Christ, the church. "Day by day the Lord added to their number those who were being saved" (Acts 2:47). It is God who saves; it is God who adds to the church.

God has become our salvation through divine incarnation in the person of the Son, in whose body a complete sacrifice was made for our sins. Jesus has become our salvation because his love reaches even to us in the depths of our wretchedness. He has become our salvation by clothing our souls in his own beautiful righteousness.

For all of us, the witness leading to redemption comes directly or indirectly from the community of those who believe. Jesus entrusted the future of Christian witness in the world to the disciples he called and taught. It is to them and, now, to us that he gave the responsibility to go "make disciples of all nations, baptizing them in the name of the Father and of the Son and of the Holy Spirit, and teaching them to obey everything that I have commanded you" (Matt 28:19–20).

The church is the community of the redeemed. As the visible agent of redemption through Jesus Christ, it serves the world around it and those within it. Faith in Jesus saves, not faith in the church, but Paul reminds us of the crucial importance of the church in the plan of redemption:

> Everyone who calls on the name of the Lord shall be saved.
>
> But how are they to call on one in whom they have not believed? And how are they to believe in one of whom they have never heard? And how are they to hear without someone to proclaim him? And how are they to proclaim him unless they are sent? As it is written, "How beautiful are the feet of those who bring good news!"
>
> (Romans 10:13–15)

Teachers play a critical role in the church's redemptive work. Through their relationships and in the content of their teaching, their service proclaims Christ. Teaching is an act that calls and enables others to hear of the one in whom they are called to believe. The teacher's own testimony is therefore an occasion of grace.

Teachers do not serve alone. Pastors, persons of prayer, saints of the church both old and young, parents, and life in the Christian community all come to bear on the life and faith of each member of the congregation. Individually and collectively the church's life speaks of Christ. Through the corporate and individual actions of its people, the members of Christ's body, Christ is made known.

Paul explained his own participation in the community that is the church. "Thanks be to God, who in Christ always leads us in triumphal procession, and through us spreads in every place the fragrance that comes from knowing him. For we are the aroma of Christ to God among those who are being saved and among those who are perishing" (2 Cor 2:14–15). Note that Paul uses the phrase "*being* saved" (emphasis added). Our own salvation is a process, a pilgrimage. In our initial commitment to Christ we find the forgiveness for sin and newness of life that accompany our conversion. Born into Christ as spiritual infants, we grow in grace and knowledge toward maturity. Gifts for the body are added to our lives. As we develop those gifts, we become more able servants of God.

Growth in Christ and the Spirit leads to the maturity of their activity in our lives. Paul referred to this maturity as the "harvest of the Spirit" (Gal 5:22, NEB). We, then, not only receive grace, we become graceful. In this process the witness of the church catches fire and serves as a beacon light to the world around it. The light shines as brightly as the burning brands of its individual members. Churches where the Spirit has no harvest fall short of their role as agents of redemption. Church life becomes commonplace. The congregation becomes a people who go through the motions of life together without acknowledging that the Christ in their midst wishes to remake them and through them remake the world. The church at Laodicea (see Rev 3:14–20) serves as a picture of the terrible fate of congregations who, resting on their laurels, simply go through the motions of church.

Much of the Western world has forgotten its need of

redemption. It thinks all it needs is a little reorientation, a little counseling, and a little more positive thinking. What humans have always needed is radical change—the transforming presence of Jesus Christ. That radical change springs from the source of life itself and must be engaged within a community married to Christ himself. Life springing from Jesus does not drive us apart; it always brings us together. God's redemption brings unity, making us one with Christ and with each other.

5.12 Community and the Channel of Redemption

The Apostle Paul frequently uses a teaching device that Bible scholars refer to as "the Pauline indicative-imperative." Paul often follows up indicative statements with moral exhortations. For instance, he says,

> Therefore, do not let sin exercise dominion in your mortal bodies, to make you obey their passions. No longer present your members to sin as instruments of wickedness, but present yourselves to God as those who have been brought from death to life, and present your members to God as instruments of righteousness. For sin will have no dominion over you, since you are not under the law but under grace.
>
> (Romans 6:12–14)

The last clause of verse 14— "since you are not under law but under grace"— states what is now actually the case, that is, the indicative: Christians *are* under grace rather than law. This statement serves as the foundation for a string of commands—the imperatives—that precede the "since": "do not let sin exercise dominion"; "no longer present your members to sin"; "present yourselves to God." The empowering grace of God available through the presence of the Holy Spirit is the crucial spiritual resource that empowers Christians to live up to the Pauline imperatives. Salvation goes beyond forgiveness and rescue to a wholeness that keeps us from repeatedly breaking our relationships with others and with God. In that sense we are always being saved.

The Christian community participates in this ongoing redemption. We need each other even as the individual parts of our body depend upon each other for the well-being of the entire body. Christians, members of Christ's body, need each other for mutual support, prayer, encouragement, nurture, and accountability. The church is God's creation. Individual people are rescued from a sinful world to become members of the body of Christ, God's new people, God's new way of being together as a community of the redeemed.

Dietrich Bonhoeffer's book *Life Together* celebrates the grace of the Christian community as it guides Christians in their common life. Bonhoeffer explained relationships, specified our mutual expectations, and helped to define what Christians should provide one another in the church.

> God has willed that we should seek and find His living Word in the witness of a brother .... as a bearer and proclaimer of the divine word of salvation.... That also clarifies the goal of all Christian community: they meet one another as bringers of the message of salvation. As such, God permits them to meet together and gives them community.... The community of Christians springs from the Biblical and Reformation message of ... justification ... through grace alone; this alone is the basis of the longing of Christians for one another.[2]

The church serves as a channel or conduit for the redemption of the world around it. The vital church—focused on its Lord and in harmony with one another—brings forth fruit.

Jesus said that he came to seek and to save the lost. The church cannot be truly focused on Jesus and the redemption he offers without becoming keenly aware of his desire to reach those who have not yet believed. The Bible tells us that "the Lord is not slow about his promise, as some think of slowness, but is patient with you, not wanting any to perish, but all to come to repentance" (2 Pet 3:9). Hundreds of millions are perishing while we are being saved. The church is God's instrument to reach them.

Many gifts and factors—witness, prayer, teaching, example, encouragement, and support—join to reach a person with the salvation offered in Christ. Only the church brings these gifts together. Only the church is adequate to function as Jesus' body.

Teachers are in a key position to make redemption possible. Christ is the Savior of the world and the Savior of each person, one at a time. A called, gifted, and mature teacher stands in Christ's stead. Each time she teaches she has the opportunity to extend the grace of Jesus. The greatest joy of a teacher is to participate in the salvation of a class member, made possible through Christ's redeeming sacrifice. The second greatest joy of a teacher is to see her student become a teacher himself.

5.2 The Church and Revelation

Matthew's Gospel recounts a moment when Jesus and the disciples were traveling through the district of Caesarea Philippi and he asked them, "Who do you say that I am?" He had already asked them what the people in the crowd were saying about him. Many rumors circulated about Jesus, and the disciples reported what people were saying: some thought that Jesus was the beheaded John the Baptist come back to life; others believed him to be the Elijah—forerunner of the Messiah; and others believed him to be the reborn spirit of Jeremiah or one of the other great prophets of Israel. Then Jesus asked his disciples a much more personal question—"Who do you say that I am?" Peter is the one to answer, "You are the Messiah, the Son of the living God." Jesus then pronounces Peter as blessed, "For flesh and blood has not revealed this to you, but my Father in heaven" (see Matt 16:13–20). Peter's statement is the product of God's revelation. Something formerly secret or unknown has been disclosed. The incident at Caesarea Philippi is a moment of divine self-disclosure.

The church is founded on God's revealing activity. The church therefore both receives and proclaims God's revelation. Revelation comes to us by the Holy Spirit. The Bible itself is quickened in our minds and hearts by the Spirit. The Spirit communes with us when we pray. The Spirit answers from within whenever we hear God's word.

> These things God has revealed to us through the Spirit; for the Spirit searches everything, even the depths of God. For what human being knows what is truly human except the human spirit that is within? So also no one comprehends what is truly God's except the Spirit of God. Now we have received not the spirit of the world, but the Spirit that is from God, so that we may understand the gifts bestowed on us by God. And we speak of these things in words not taught by human wisdom but taught by the Spirit, interpreting spiritual things to those who are spiritual.
>
> (1 Corinthians 2:10–13)

173

In our effort to live faithfully to God, we can trust God to be faithful by granting the Holy Spirit to us. The Spirit will go before us, travel with us, and remain after us. Our roles are those of witness, proclamation, and teaching. The Holy Spirit will authenticate what we say in the experience of those to whom we witness.

God is revealed as we function together as the body of Christ. In worship, through prayer, thanksgiving, praise, singing, listening to the sermon and the reading of scripture, God speaks to us. God speaks of ancient people and ways. God reminds us that divine work spans time, reaching back and ahead. God speaks to us of our lives in the Christian community, that is, the church. Wisdom, guidance, and peace are revealed and received in community.

The same is true in our classrooms. In addition to wisdom, guidance, and peace, we receive "instruction in righteousness" (2 Tim 3:16). Our teaching task is to bring the testimony of scripture to bear on the life stories of our students within the influence of the Holy Spirit. We need not be fearful in this. The Holy Spirit plays the major role, including giving us the gifts of teaching. We must take our responsibility seriously. The gifts must be "stirred up" or developed (2 Tim 1:6). Planning, availability, genuine concern, study of scripture—all prepare us for teaching. Prayer prepares us to meet our students. Together the disciplines of the teacher free the Holy Spirit among us to reveal God.

5.21 The Teacher's Disciplines

• Availability is the first discipline of the teacher

God uses persons who make themselves available for service. God is one who seeks out and calls to those who are willing to know and do the will of God. At the heart of availability is the life of prayer and service.

• Prayer is the second discipline of the teacher

Prayer is conversing with God. Through prayer God shapes us to think God's thoughts. Much public prayer consists of thanking God for intervening on our behalf and asking for direction and guidance. Personal prayer includes thanks for God's goodness. Jesus himself encouraged us to ask for what we need. Prayer should also include thinking about our lives and our life situations while intentionally seeking the presence of God. Prayer includes listening and loving; it may include laughing and crying. Prayer should include time in the scriptures, listening to the stories of God's people in the presence of the God who intervened on their behalf.

As teachers we can present each of our students to God. We can allow God to bring us closer together, to show us how we can help each one grow and mature. Prayer brings clarity and resolve. Prayer directs us and steadies us. Prayer gives us courage and patience. Prayer reveals God to us. Through prayer we find God in us.

• Bible study is the third discipline of the teacher

While we read the scripture devotionally as part of prayer, we have the opportunity also to be students of the Word. The Bible has been preserved and cherished for our sake across thousands of years. The story of scripture reveals the testimonies of those who served God. As teachers the Bible is our primary tangible resource. The more we learn its stories, the more we learn about it, the better God is able to use us.

• The fourth discipline of the teacher is the study of her class

The teacher reflects on each individual member of the class. Who is he? Who is she? What are their lives like? What do they need? What challenges do they face? Where are they in their development? In their passages of life?

• The fifth discipline of the teacher is to see congruence

At the heart of the teacher's role is the responsibility to be accountable before God and learners for how the teacher lives out what is taught. The authority of Jesus rested in this reality: he lived what he taught. The authority of any teacher rests in the same reality.

The church is the recipient of divine revelation and the proclaimer of what is revealed. This is a matter of balance. Proclamation is an essential role, but if the revelation is not lived out, the power of testimony and witness weakens. Sadly, the church most often thinks of itself as the proclaimer of the revelation of God on Sunday morning or whenever the word is proclaimed through the act of preaching. Ironically this makes the church both the recipient of God's revealing work *and* the audience for its own proclamation. For many congregations the proclamation of revelation occurs primarily within the walls of the church buildings. This proclamation cannot be overvalued, but the church has another responsibility—to proclaim the word of God to the world around it.

Jesus told his disciples that they were to be salt and leaven to a needy world. They were to be a city set on a hill that could not be hidden. The church is God's voice confronting sin in society while proclaiming God's concern for the poor, the hungry, and the imprisoned. This theme pervades the gospels and is best seen in Jesus' own ministry, the ministry of healing, wholeness, and reconciliation. This ministry now rests in the custody of the church. As the church goes about the ministry of reconciliation, it witnesses to the reign of God that was incarnate in its Lord. Such witness reveals God to the world. The most succinct overall description of the church's work in the world is found in the scripture that Jesus himself claimed for his own ministry:

> The Spirit of the Lord is upon me, because he has
>   anointed me to bring good news to the poor.
> He has sent me to proclaim release to the captives and
>   recovery of sight to the blind, to let the oppressed
>   go free,
> to proclaim the acceptable year of the Lord.
>
> (Luke 4:18–19)

The teacher's role is seldom proclamation in the sense of preaching. Instead the teacher is to teach the justice and mercy of God as set forth in the stories of scripture, and to help students think about their own and the church's responsibility to live out that divine justice and mercy in their daily lives.

5.3 Church as the Community of Christ

Koinonia is one of the key words of the New Testament. It refers to the fellowship or communion based in the love that Christians have for one another. It is expressed in the common activities of the body—corporate worship (especially the ordinance of the Lord's Supper), common meals, the work and play of the group as a whole. In the New Testament *koinonia* is a word of uncommon richness, combining the potent ideas of friendship and fellowship.

> Christian fellowship is based on the believer's primary relationship to Jesus Christ, the crucified and Risen Lord, who is spiritually present in the church, which is declared to be his body and all believers to be limbs of that body. Fellowship is then a sharing of the faithful's communion with Christ and with one another and, therefore, is a common participation spiritually that leads to close social interaction and mutual service.[3]

Koinonia expresses the fundamental dynamic of the church's life as the community of Christ.

5.31 Jesus Prayed for the Community of His Followers

Atonement and reconciliation are at the heart of God's work as revealed in scripture. From the beginning God has been calling and forming a people to restore them to a righteous relationship with God and one another—a people who will faithfully witness to God's love and goodness. *Koinonia* is one of the few New Testament words that encompasses that divine purpose. James Massey strongly emphasizes the fellowship of the Christian community:

> In speaking of community, I am using a word of great depth and dimension. In some ways it is an even stronger word than church.... Christian community is the bringing together of persons whose lives have been touched and changed by Christ. His life and work are the basis for the bond between believers, and his Spirit seeks always to promote experiences of that bond in personal openness and regard for each other.[4]

The Gospel of John recounts Jesus' own impassioned plea for the community of his disciples beginning with chapter 13.

I give you a new commandment, that you love one another. Just as I have loved you, you also should love one another. By this everyone will know that you are my disciples, if you have love for one another.

(John 13:34–35)

On that day you will know that I am in my Father, and you in me, and I in you.

(14:20)

I ask not only on behalf of these, but also on behalf of those who will believe in me through their word, that they may all be one. As you, Father, are in me and I am in you, may they also be in us, so that the world may believe that you have sent me.

(17:20–21)

Whatever structure the church takes on, however it chooses to worship, whatever kind of buildings it builds, and whatever organizations it launches, Jesus will not be content until we are one and bound together by our love for one another in him. Nor will Jesus be satisfied with a lip service that says we love people spiritually but don't like them personally. Jesus expected that our love would be so self-evident that outsiders will recognize it and name it.

Clearly the Bible teaches that unity is a gift of God, extended to all who experience salvation through Jesus Christ. It is a free gift of God provided by Jesus' death on the cross. That salvation, however, does not really do a person any good until that person responds in faith to Jesus and actualizes that salvation.

In the same sense, unity must also be actualized in the life of the congregation as a visible expression of the Christian community. No greater challenge presented itself to the churches of the New Testament era than the temptation to disunity. Ethnic differences repeatedly threatened to divide early

Christian churches. The great story of Peter's vision and subsequent meeting with Cornelius the centurion (Acts
9:32–10:48) illustrates both the depth of the problem and
God's insistence that the people of God overcome it as a unified community of Christian fellowship and love.

Jews and Gentiles rarely entered into one another's worlds.
They were rigidly separated by years of mutual suspicion and
mistrust. Very different customs, traditions, and dietary regulations also served to build up a wall of separation and hostil-
ity between Jew and Gentile. As the early church spread and
Gentiles began to be converted to Jesus, it became increasingly clear to the leaders of the Jesus movement that these
barriers would have to be broken down. The Acts narrative
demonstrates how clearly that vision was made to Peter. In
this famous story, God grants Peter permission to eat from a
group of animals that Jews believed were unclean. To eat
them violated the Deuteronomic code. To Peter's initial
denial and claim to be obedient to the dietary laws, the voice
in the vision replies, "What God has made clean, you must
not call profane" (Acts 11:9).

This vision is the prelude to eventual meeting of Cornelius
and Peter, a meeting where Peter says of his new Gentile
brothers and sisters, "If then God gave them the same gift that
he gave us when we believed in the Lord Jesus Christ, who
was I that I could hinder God?" (Acts 11:17). This question
silenced Peter's critics, at least for the moment, but the challenge of Jew and Gentile finding common fellowship continued to confront the church as it determined to be God's community of Christian love and unity.

The gift of unity comes to life in the community of believers found in a local congregation. Over time we become
bound to each other by the chords woven in the experiences

we pass through together in fellowship with Christ. Not all of those experiences are enjoyable; many are difficult. Occasionally we all create difficulty for others and for the church.

In times of difficulty we need each other more than at other times. We need each other more critically when we are at fault. The weak rely on the strong to pull them through the difficult times. Paradoxically, however, the strong may need the weak more than the weak need the strong. Thinking of ourselves as strong may lead us to think we are doing God's work in our own strength. The weaker brother or sister reminds us of our own frailty. The Apostle Paul explains:

> But God chose what is foolish in the world to shame the wise; God chose what is weak in the world to shame the strong; God chose what is low and despised in the world, things that are not, to reduce to nothing things that are, so that no one might boast in the presence of God. He is the source of your life in Christ Jesus, who became for us wisdom from God, and righteousness and sanctification and redemption, in order that, as it is written, "Let the one who boasts, boast in the Lord."
>
> (1 Corinthians 1:27–30)

If we exclude the weaker brother, the poorer sister, and the stranger, we run the risk of excluding Jesus from our community. Often, scripture tells us, Jesus comes to us in the guise of the poor sister, the unlovely brother, and the stranger. Jesus himself reminds us, "Truly I tell you, just as you did it to one of the least of these ... you did it to me" (Matt 25:40). Community is a gift of God, but it is built slowly, brick by brick. Time, commitment to our common Lord, and mutual experience form the ties that are the means by which we become the answer to Jesus' prayer that we all may be one.

In like manner congregations relate to other congregations in a larger community that is equally necessary for Christian unity. Congregations, like individual Christians, experience emotional highs and lows. Congregations seek aid from each other to complete united missions, to prepare leaders, to raise funds, and to provide prayer support. This gift of unity also needs actualization. Some congregations may think, for a time, that they have become self-sufficient and independent. The phrases "independent Christian" or "independent church" are oxymorons. All Christian community is dependent upon the Spirit of Christ and the love of other believers. We cannot serve Christ alone. Again, the weak need the strong; the strong need the weak.

The role of teachers in community is indispensable. Community strengthens and deepens as individual members are nurtured and mature. This is the teacher's task. Just as Christ gifts teachers, so teachers call forth the gifts Christ gives to the learner. As the learners develop their gifts, under the teacher's guidance and support, they take their place in the body. The whole body is strengthened, producing fruit. This fruit is new Christians. As the community nurtures these tender new shoots of the kingdom, it realizes more and more the dawning kingdom of God to which its own actions witness.

5.4 The Church and Discipleship

When the Apostle Paul said "we," he spoke for and of a community of moral expectation in which Christian character is formed and cultivated. The result of this process of formation and cultivation, then and now, is mature followers of Jesus, Christian disciples. One can think of many of Paul's letters as efforts to discipline his congregations, bringing their discipleship into fuller expression. Paul's letter to the Galatian Christians especially illustrates this point. They had fallen under the influence of a group of teachers who interpret the relationship of Jesus' followers to Jewish law very differently than did Paul.

When he learns of this new idea, loose among the Galatians, Paul writes to them in strong, disciplining words, "You foolish Galatians! Who has bewitched you?" (3:1). Later he says, "You were running well; who prevented you from obeying the truth?" (5:7).... "For you were called to freedom, brothers and sisters; only do not use your freedom as an opportunity for self-indulgence, but through love become slaves to one another. For the whole law is summed up in a single commandment, 'You shall love your neighbor as yourself' " (5:13–14). Paul is a model of the Christian teacher at work, upbraiding, chastising, encouraging, and clarifying. Why? That these young Galatian Christians might grow as disciples. The church is a community of discipleship.

5.41 Discipleship and Discipline

Those whom God calls and sets apart receive the gifts of the Holy Spirit. They not only receive them, they develop and use them for the good of the whole church. Such persons become true disciples as they reach spiritual maturity. Discipleship empowers the church. The church cannot be effective if persons are not maturing as disciples. To be a disciple of Jesus is to be a follower of Jesus.

Discipleship and discipline share a common linguistic root—*discipulous,* meaning pupil. The origin of this word may be the Latin *discipere,* meaning to grasp and comprehend. The idea, then, behind discipleship is that a disciple is one who is willing and able to put himself or herself under a discipline in order to learn from a teacher.

Discipline often carries unpleasant connotations with it. Persons may think of parents or other authorities whose discipline seemed excessive. They may link the word discipline to painful experiences. While discipline may involve pain, it is more likely a response to pain than synonymous with pain. Discipline must not be avoided. There is no accomplishment without it.

> The meaning of discipline for the life of godliness is taught quite clearly in the biblical tradition. Discipline is education; it is what results when we properly respond in accepting and obeying that which instructs and cultivates us for the concerns and issues of a godly life.[5]

The disciplines of the Christian life provide God with the opportunity to shape our living. All the disciplines turn the individual Christian and Christians together toward God. They interrupt our lives with divine encounter. Through discipline we find our lives transformed from the secular to the sacred. Discipline fits us to bear the name of Jesus. Through discipline we learn obedience. The first letter of Peter mentions discipline three different times in its brief pages (see 1:13, 4:7, 5:8). This discipline prepares the believer for service and action, to face opposition, and to order the believer's life in humility.

As teachers we fulfill our roles as we demonstrate discipline in our lives and call those we teach into holy discipline. It is not our job to bring trials and tribulations upon our students, but we are in a position to help them deal with the difficulties that inevitably arise in their lives. Even better, we can help them develop the disciplines that make it possible to deal with challenge and difficulty when they do arrive.

Discipline first comes from without. Then, as we mature, disciplines become internalized. As spiritual children we receive from God external guidance through parents and teachers. As our relationship with God matures the disciplines of the Spirit become second nature. The writer to the Hebrews reminds us that this discipline emerges from God:

> Endure trials for the sake of discipline. God is treating you as children; for what child is there whom a parent does not discipline? If you do not have that discipline in which all children share, then you are illegitimate and not his children. Moreover, we had human parents to discipline us, and we respected them. Should we not be even more willing to be subject to the Father of spirits and live? For they disciplined us for a short time as seemed best to them, but he disciplines us for our good, in order that we may share his holiness. Now, discipline always seems painful rather than pleasant at the time, but later it yields the peaceful fruit of righteousness to those who have been trained by it.
>
> (Hebrews 12:7–11)

The disciplines of the church are both communal and private. The private and the communal confirm each other. One's personal relationship with God enriches the whole life of the community. The personal disciplines are study, devotion (including meditation and prayer), and fasting. The communal disciplines are study and worship.

Some folks say that they don't need church; they can find God in creation—the mountains, the stars, the beauty of nature. Others look for God only in the walled confines of the sanctuary and fail to meet God in every avenue of life. Both are short-sighted. We need solitude, but to grow as disciples of the Lord Jesus we need the Christian community. The name of this community of discipline and moral expectation is church.

5.42 Discipleship and Devotion

The disciplined life within the Christian community is nourished by the private devotional life of its members. Two such private disciplines include prayer and fasting.

• Discipleship and Prayer

Most Christians pray. We pray because we have been taught that it is one of the main sources of growth and power in a Christian's life. We pray because we find many biblical examples of men and women of God who prayed often and with great depth of feeling and communion. For many Christians prayer is a daily habit: at meals, when we go to bed, in church, and, fervently, in desperate situations. Many feel guilty about their prayer lives. It's not regular enough, long enough, or spiritual enough. Guilt results from the unrealistic ideals of what prayer should be. Many have been told about Martin Luther who is supposed to have said, "I have so much to do today that I must pray at least seven hours." Or perhaps we've heard of E. Stanley Jones who spent two hours in prayer every evening—even when he was a guest at someone's dinner party.

Vital prayer is conversation with God. There are two aspects to this conversation—speaking and listening, for conversation implies two-way communication. When we become conscious of the constant presence of God, it becomes natural to speak to God as we would speak to a good friend and companion. This form of prayer is often casual and unplanned—the way we speak to a spouse, a coworker, or a golf partner. Yet all forms of prayer have value. If prayer is limited to perfunctory habit, it has merit because our habits help shape us. If prayer is a recitation of psalms and other readings to God, it has merit because the great thoughts of others can help us form our thoughts and voice our needs and hopes.

The more we develop a conversational relationship with God, the more we find meaning in planned prayer times. When we talk to God while driving, washing dishes, or riding on an elevator, we are much more likely to have something to say to God when we do try to pray for half an hour. The goal for the disciple is focused intimate involvement with God in every aspect of our lives. God is eager to be a part of our lives. God waits only for our invitation.

At the same time, in this intimacy with God one does not cozy up with God as one might with a cuddly teddy bear. God is still I AM WHO I AM.

Jurgen Moltmann warns us,

> To know God means to suffer God, and anyone who "suffers" God experiences the reversal of his existence, the pains of his life's rebirth.... He dies, as Paul says, to the demands and compulsions of "this world" and awakes to new life for God and his kingdom.[6]

Our personal focus on God will undo and redo us in the image of Christ. It is a dangerous business. It is the business of personal renewal that will unleash the power of the Holy Spirit in us and in those we teach.

Effective teachers model a lifestyle of intimacy with God. They share out of their own rich experience. Students do not

begin with hour-long quiet times at 4:00 A.M. A good beginning includes a planned time with a brief passage of scripture
as a thought starter, a few minutes of spoken prayer, a few
moments of listening, and closing with a psalm of praise.
Encourage beginners to speak their prayer aloud even though
they are alone. They may state requests, speak candidly about
questions of faith and life, even about doubts. Reflection over
the tasks of the day, and a short period of silence for listening
provide a conclusion. Regular attendance upon God is more
important than length.

• Discipleship and Fasting

To a greater or lesser degree, the life of devotional prayer
is expected of every Christian. Not so with fasting. Fasting is
a voluntary and private discipline. Jesus clearly taught that
fasting is to be done in secret. In a congregation where many
are fasting no one will know it. Since the discipline of fasting
cannot be learned by observing models, teaching the discipline of fasting acquires a greater importance. While a community, a congregation, or a family may invite members to
fast, the fast is to remain a secret rite. It loses its benefit in the
public eye.

There are at least four reasons Christians practice the discipline of fasting: for discernment, for preparation, for power,
and for intimacy. Across the centuries when God's people
face the need to make a crucial decision, they often choose to
fast and pray until the will of God becomes clear.

Acts 13 gives us an example.

Inexperienced leaders of an infant church were gathered at
Antioch. God had brought a church together there, and many
had been converted and baptized. A number of the leaders
were fasting and praying when the Holy Spirit spoke to them

saying, "Set apart for me Barnabas and Saul for the work to which I have called them" (13:2). After more prayer and fasting, the church commissioned Barnabas and Saul for missionary service and sent them off with their blessing and support. They had discerned God's next step and followed it in faith, buttressed by their clear understanding that what they were to do was God's leading. In the process, Antioch became the first missionary church.

In other biblical cases the discipline of fasting supports people who already have discerned what it is that God calls them to do. They fast and pray in preparation. A powerful example of this kind of fasting is found in the Old Testament Book of Esther.

The Persian king Ahasuerus noticed the great beauty of Esther and made her his queen. The King of Persia enjoyed absolute power of life and death over all of his subjects and no one, including Queen Esther, was permitted to come before the king unless summoned; summary execution awaited anyone bold enough to enter the king's presence unbidden. The king had an official named Haman who was a rival of Esther's uncle and adopted father, Mordecai. Haman plotted to destroy both Mordecai and Esther by getting the king to give him authority to destroy all Jews. Unknown to either Haman or even Ahasuerus, Queen Esther was a Jewess.

Esther finally decided she must take the case of her people before the king, but the king did not call for her. The situation became urgent. She decided she must risk her life by entering the king's presence without a royal summons. To prepare for this act of extraordinary courage she fasted three days. When she came before the king, she won his favor. The story is much longer, but ultimately Esther's action and bravery saved her uncle and her people from certain annihilation.

The discipline of fasting also fosters the growth of spiritual power in individual believers. When Jesus' disciples were unable to cast out a demon, Jesus responded, "This kind can come forth by nothing but by prayer and fasting" (Mark 9:29, KJV). Fasting provides no magic potion but does prepare one spiritually. It is a form of purification so that God is able to work more powerfully through that person.

The primary purpose of the discipline of fasting is to move disciples toward a greater intimacy with God.

> There was also a prophet, Anna the daughter of Phanuel, of the tribe of Asher. She was of a great age, having lived with her husband seven years after her marriage, then as a widow to the age of eighty-four. She never left the temple but worshiped there with fasting and prayer night and day. At that moment she came, and began to praise God and to speak about the child to all who were looking for the redemption of Jerusalem.
>
> (Luke 2:36–38)

Anna's intimacy with God prepared her to recognize the Messiah when she saw him as an infant. Jesus also fasted to prepare himself for the difficult mission that lay ahead. After his baptism by John, Jesus went alone into the wilderness to fast and pray in preparation to face the ordeal of his temptations and to be ready to begin his public ministry (see Luke 4).

Fasting should never be an occasion for exhibition, self-destruction, or manipulation. Jesus strongly condemned religious leaders of his day who, by dress and activity, made sure all knew that they were fasting:

> And whenever you fast, do not look dismal, like the hypocrites, for they disfigure their faces so as to show

others that they are fasting. Truly I tell you, they have
received their reward. But when you fast, put oil on your
head and wash your face, so that your fasting may be
seen not by others but by your Father who is in secret;
and your Father who sees in secret will reward you
(Matthew 6:16–18)

5.43 Discipleship and Worship

The disciplined life within the Christian community is a
combination of personal and private devotion and public and
communal worship.

The Letter to the Hebrews encourages its readers to
"consider how to provoke one another to good deeds, not
neglecting to meet together, as is the habit of some, but
encouraging one another, and all the more as you see the Day
approaching" (Heb 10:24–25). If prayer and fasting are private forms of Christian discipline, then worship will be one
of its public and corporate forms.

In the very first place, worship is the acknowledgment that
the God of Abraham, Isaac, Jacob, Esther, Rahab, Jesus,
Mary, Peter, and Paul is the only God of the universe.
Worship focuses on God. It brings us to God. We admit our
human frailty, our utter dependence on God's mercy and
grace. We declare our love for God and our intent to be obedient. We offer praise and thanksgiving in celebration for
what God has done for us.

The elements that comprise and form the centrality of
Christian worship are adoration and praise, confession and
petition, assurance of pardon and God's faithfulness, proclamation of God's word, and the human response in obedience
and commitment. Worship that includes these elements will
likely be whole and good. Worship that consistently focuses
on specific items of these elements while excluding others

will mislead worshipers in their understanding of who God is, how God wishes to relate to them, and how God expects the people of God to live. Good teaching prepares students to participate in the elements of worship within the classroom, at home, and especially in the larger context of the congregation's corporate worship.

The worship practices of the church include common events, some of which are called ordinances. Three of these—baptism, communion, and foot washing—are older than the New Testament itself, dating back to the very events to which the New Testament witnesses. God's grace is supplied to the believer individually and to the church collectively as we faithfully observe these practices that Jesus himself commanded us to do. Symbolic in nature, these ordinances are full of rich meaning, reminding us of the work that God has done and is doing among us.

• The Ordinance of Baptism

Baptism is the basic Christian rite of passage. While baptism does not make one a Christian, it serves a critical role in the life of the believer. In baptism we celebrate our death to sin through Jesus' death and our resurrection to new life through the risen Lord. The practice is fundamental to all Christians. To forsake it is an act of separation from all who are Christian. Theologically speaking, baptism is connected with the Christian hope of resurrection. All the ordinances, in fact, are tied to this future hope. Participation in them symbolically expresses the disciple's hope in God's future. "As many of you as were baptized into Christ have clothed yourselves with Christ. There is no longer Jew or Greek, there is no longer slave or free, there is no longer male and female; for all of you are one in Christ Jesus" (Gal 3:27–28).

• The Ordinance of Communion

Christians of nearly all theological persuasions share more common interpretations of Communion than they do of baptism. Communion, the Lord's Supper, connects us to Jesus' death. As Paul states, we "proclaim the Lord's death until he returns" (1 Cor 11:26). The symbol of the broken bread is linked to Jesus' broken body on the cross. The juice or wine represents Jesus' blood that was spilled that we might be saved. We remember—and celebrate—not only the death but the bitter nature of that death as we remember our utter dependence on Jesus' saving action.

In the Lord's Supper, we also commune with those who presently serve Jesus, those who have gone before, and those who will come after. Communion is a true celebration of the unity of the church that spans all time—past, present, and future. Partaking of communion we claim our victory in Jesus, our oneness in him, our willingness to embrace our own death, and our hope to be ultimately united with him and all who are his.

• The Ordinance of Foot Washing

Foot washing is practiced by a minority of church groups. Its character, however, is rooted deeply in the witness of Jesus himself. His words echo across the centuries: "If I, your Lord and Teacher, have washed your feet, you also ought to wash one another's feet." (See John 13:1–17.) The intimacy of this act is at the heart of its meaning for individual believers and the church. God invades our privacy and breaks down walls of distinction among the people of God. Foot washing symbolizes what God has done and is doing among us as we are called to be like the humble Son of Man, defining the church in terms of lowly servanthood.

5.44 Discipleship and Study

The life of discipleship is a life of study. This study is not limited to preachers, professors, theologians, biblical scholars, and teachers. All are called to study at a level appropriate to their own calling and gifts. Paul's words to Timothy are pertinent to all who seek to grow as disciples of the Lord Jesus Christ:

> But as for you, continue in what you have learned and firmly believed, knowing from whom you learned it, and how from childhood you have known the sacred writings that are able to instruct you for salvation through faith in Christ Jesus. All scripture is inspired by God and is useful for teaching, for reproof, for correction, and for training in righteousness, so that every one who belongs to God may be equipped for every good work.
>
> (2 Timothy 3:14–17)

Reading the Bible devotionally provides a beginning, but if we are to take this book seriously, we will become students of the word, so that we may also be doers of the word. All who are Christian should know some basics about the Bible— where it came from, what kinds of culture gave it birth, its history, and the variety of its forms.

We have already mentioned the clear expectation in the Great Commission that those who make disciples will teach. They will teach all that the Lord has commanded them. Making disciples is the call. Conversion begins the process. Learning continues it. Each congregation and pastor is responsible for those entrusted to their care. We need a planned approach to see that each Christian has the opportunity to hear the call to grow and develop, to become a disciple, a mature follower of Jesus. In this connection a curriculum is critical. A curriculum is not the individual pieces handed out in the classroom. A curriculum is the plan that stands behind the material and coordinates it in a systematic manner so that individuals can count on learning and growing in the whole counsel of God.

5.5 The Life of the Church

The church brings everything together. It is Jesus' own body on earth. It is the seed of the kingdom itself and—like all seeds—it includes in its heart the earnest of the kingdom that will be made manifest at Christ's return. The church provides the foundation upon which Christians can stand. It is a stable island in the swiftly running and changing river of life.

The practices of the church bring wholeness to brokenness, healing to diseased persons, and hope to every situation, no matter how helpless. The church is God's great gift to us. It is ours to cherish. It is ours to love. It is ours to serve. It is, of course, impossible to be a committed church with uncommitted members. Much of the uniqueness of Christianity consists in the fact that simple people can be amazingly powerful when they are members one of another. This affirms once again that we really do need each other.

Teachers play a critical role in the health of the church.

The effectiveness of the local congregation is in direct proportion to the effectiveness of its teachers. When teachers accept their roles, when they shoulder their responsibilities, and when they understand their role in the God-ordained process of discipleship, the people of God move more consistently toward maturity and bring in much fruit, that is, new Christians.

> About this we have much to say that is hard to explain, since you have become dull in understanding. For though by this time you ought to be teachers, you need someone to teach you again the basic elements of the oracles of God. You need milk, not solid food; for everyone who lives on milk, being still an infant, is unskilled in the word of righteousness. But solid food is for the mature, for those whose faculties have been trained by practice to distinguish good from evil.

> Therefore let us go on toward perfection, leaving behind the basic teaching about Christ, and not laying again the foundation: repentance from dead works and faith toward God, instruction about baptisms, laying on of hands, resurrection of the dead, and eternal judgment. And we will do this, if God permits.

> (Hebrews 5:11—6:3)

Notes

1. James Earl Massey, *Concerning Christian Unity* (Anderson, Ind: Warner Press, 1979), 11.

2. Bonhoeffer, 23.

3. s.v. "Fellowship" in *The Dictionary of Bible and Religion* (Nashville: Abingdon, 1986), 357.

4. James Earl Massey, *The Hidden Disciplines* (Anderson, Ind: Warner Press, 1972), 11–14.

5. Massey, *The Hidden Disciplines,* 11.

6. Jurgen Moltmann, *The Church in the Power of the Spirit* (New York: Harper and Row, 1977), 283.

Works cited

Blenkinsopp. 1983. *A History of Prophecy* in Israel. Philadelphia: Westminster Press.

Bonhoeffer, Dietrich. 1976. *Life Together.* NY: Harper and Row.

Bright, John. 1959. *A History of Israel.* Philadelphia: Westminster Press.

_____. 1953. *The Kingdom of God.* Nashville: Abingdon.

Brueggemann, Walter. 1968. *Confronting the Bible: A Resource and Discussion Book for Youth.* NY: Herder and Herder.

_____. 1990. "First and Second Samuel" in *Interpretation: A Bible Commentary for Teaching and Preaching.* Atlanta: John Knox Press.

_____. 1982. "Genesis." In *Interpretation: A Bible Commentary for Teaching and Preaching.* Atlanta: John Knox Press.

_____. 1987. *Hope Within History.* Atlanta: John Knox Press.

_____. 1993. "Jeremiah: Faithfulness in the Midst of Fickleness." In *The Newell Lectureships,* Vol II. Anderson, Ind: Warner Press.

_____. 1992. *Old Testament Theology: Essays on Structure, Theme, and Text.* Minneapolis: Fortress Press.

_____. July 1985. "Passion and Perspective: Two Dimensions of Education in the Bible." In *Theology Today.* XLII/2.

The Dictionary of Bible and Religion. 1986. Nashville: Abingdon Press. s.v. "Jehovah"

Eichrodt, Walter. 1962. *Theology of the Old Testament.* London: SCM Press.

Hauerwas, Stanley. 1981. *A Community of Character.* Notre Dame: University of Notre Dame Press.

Heschel, Abraham. 1962. *The Prophets.* NY: Harper and Row.

_____. 1955. *God in Search of Man: A Philosophy of Judaism.* NY: Harper and Row.

Interpreters' Dictionary of the Bible. 1962. Nashville: Abingdon Press. s.v. "Covenant"

_____. 1962. Nashville: Abingdon Press. s.v. "Word"

Kasemann, Ernst. 1969. *Jesus Means Freedom.* Philadelphia: Fortress.

Lampe, Peter. January 1994. "The Eucharist: Identifying with Christ on the Cross." In *Interpretation.* XLVII/1.

Massey, James Earl. 1979. *Concerning Christian Unity.* Anderson, Ind: Warner Press.

_____. 1972. *The Hidden Disciplines.* Anderson, Ind: Warner Press.

Moltmann, Jurgen. 1977. *The Church in the Power of the Spirit.* New York: Harper and Row.

Mouw, Richard. 1994. *Consulting the Faithful.* Grand Rapids: Eerdmans.

Nolan, Albert. 1976. *Jesus Before Christianity.* Philadelphia: Westminster Press.

Robinson, H. Wheeler. 1980. *Corporate Personality in Ancient Israel.* Philadelphia: Fortress.

Strege, Merle. 1993. *Tell Me Another Tale: Further Reflections on the Church of God.* Anderson, Ind: Warner Press.

_____. 1991. *Tell Me the Tale: Historical Reflections on the Church of God.* Anderson, Ind: Warner Press.

Taylor, John V. 1986. *Weep Not for Me: Meditations on the Cross and Resurrection.* Geneva, Switzerland: World Council of Churches.

Wickersham, Henry. 1894. *Holiness Bible Subjects.* Grand Junction, Mich: Gospel Trumpet Company.

Willimon, William. 1983. *The Service of God.* Nashville: Abingdon.